POLISH COOKING

POLISH COOKING

Marianna Olszewska Heberle

HPBOOKS

THE BERKLEY PUBLISHING GROUP
Published by the Penguin Group
Penguin Group (USA) Inc.
375 Hudson Street, New York, New York 10014, USA
Penguin Group (Canada), 90 Eglinton Avenue East, Suite 700, Toronto, Ontario M4P 2Y3, Canada
(a division of Pearson Penguin Canada Inc.)
Penguin Books Ltd., 80 Strand, London WC2R 0RL, England
Penguin Group Ireland, 25 St. Stephen's Green, Dublin 2, Ireland (a division of Penguin Books Ltd.)
Penguin Group (Australia), 250 Camberwell Road, Camberwell, Victoria 3124, Australia
(a division of Pearson Australia Group Pty. Ltd.)
Penguin Books India Pvt. Ltd., 11 Community Centre, Panchsheel Park, New Delhi—110 017, India
Penguin Group (NZ), cnr. Airborne and Rosedale Roads, Albany, Auckland 1310, New Zealand
(a division of Pearson New Zealand Ltd.)
Penguin Books (South Africa) (Pty.) Ltd., 24 Sturdee Avenue, Rosebank, Johannesburg 2196, South Africa
Penguin Books Ltd., Registered Offices: 80 Strand, London WC2R 0RL, England

Copyright © 2005 by Penguin Group (USA) Inc.
Text design by Diane Hobbing of SNAP-HAUS Graphics
Cover design by Liz Sheehan

The recipes contained in this book are to be followed exactly as written. The publisher is not responsible for
your specific health or allergy needs that may require medical supervision. The publisher is not responsible
for any adverse reactions to the recipes contained in this book.

PRINTING HISTORY
HPBooks trade paperback edition / December 2005

HPBooks is a registered trademark of Penguin Group (USA) Inc.

Library of Congress Cataloging-in-Publication Data

Heberle, Marianna Olszewska.
     Polish cooking / Marianna Olszewska Heberle.
         p. cm
     Originally published: Los Angeles, Calif. : HPBooks, c1991.
     Includes index.
     ISBN 1-55788-477-3 (pbk.)
     1. Cookery, Polish. I. Title.

TX723.5.P6H43 2005
641.59438—dc22

                                                                                         2005052503

PRINTED IN THE UNITED STATES OF AMERICA

10   9   8   7   6   5   4   3   2   1

CONTENTS

POLISH
COOKING

It's been twenty years since the first edition of *Polish Cooking* was prepared, and a lot has changed since then. Not, however, with most of the recipes within—they are based on traditions that are, in many cases, hundreds of years old. But change has come to Poland. Poles today are living beneath an umbrella of freedom—out from behind the restrictive and repressive influences of the old Soviet Union. Indeed, shortly after the first edition, the communist regimes of many eastern countries started falling like dominoes. Their peoples tasted freedom and democracy and formed exciting new alliances. This political revolution brought major lifestyle changes for much of Eastern Europe's population. My parents and extended family have experienced these changes firsthand. Gone are times of scarce ingredients. Today is a horn of plenty in Poland, with grocery stores and markets featuring foods and ingredients found anywhere else in Europe. Yet Poland has always been a land of strange contrasts, and continues to be so. Though much of Poland is still rural, it's now common to see on one side of a street a pair of grandparents still living in a homemade masonry and thatched-roof dwelling, performing everyday activities the same way they did in the early 1900s, while across the street a modern split-level home is occupied by a younger family enjoying all the conveniences and trappings of modern society, includ-

ing the most up-to-date computerized kitchen appliances and other labor-saving devices.

What's different with this edition of *Polish Cooking*? Apart from a new format, there are some refinements to the contents. A few recipes contain easy-to-find or substitute ingredients instead of some difficult-to-find ones. But it's certainly not a modern version of past editions. It includes over a dozen additional recipes that individuals have repeatedly asked about or requested over the years, and some of my childhood favorites that had not found their way into earlier editions. One such often-requested recipe, Czarnina, which literally translates into "Blood Soup" but is also known as "Duck

PREFACE

Soup," is admittedly an "exotic-sounding" dish, exactly the kind I said in earlier editions would not be found within these pages—but it's really not so unusual, and to leave it out at this point would have disappointed Polish old-timers.

As always, after preparing a recipe from its instructions, the next time you make it, feel free to experiment with its seasonings, cooking times, and ingredients.

Please, make these recipes yours to keep and enjoy.

Best wishes,
Marianna

Welcome to the wonderful world of Polish cuisine! If you've been here before, you know what a delicious experience it is. If you've never ventured within its boundaries, you're in for an enriching surprise.

As a result of catered "ethnic" wedding receptions and small, late-night neighborhood taverns where frozen, mass-produced *pierogies* are heated instantly in microwaves, a certain impression of Polish food has developed. Many people of Polish and non-Polish ancestry alike believe that a Polish diet consists entirely of pickles, pierogies, *golombkies*, duck soup, and *kielbasa*. That's like saying the Irish thrive only on potatoes and soda bread, or the Germans on sauerkraut and *hasenpfeffer*.

INTRODUCTION

You're going to discover that Polish cookery is not so characteristic as the cuisine of other nations, such as the Chinese, French, or Italian. While steeped in tradition, Polish cooking also has been strongly influenced by outside forces. People are going to eat whatever they like and whatever is available. They don't particularly care if it's indigenous to Poland. If they prefer a kind of soup more commonly prepared in Russia, they're going to eat that without a passing thought as to where the recipe originated. They simply like good food prepared tastefully. That's what the recipes in this book are all about.

They're what the Poles of today are eating. Together, the dishes are representative of the fare found in over 90 percent of the country's homes and restaurants.

But lest you be deceived, this book is not a catchall encyclopedia of every dish prepared in Poland. During the volume's assembly, equal time was spent deciding which recipes to exclude. The criteria for selecting each dish were that the recipe had to be both appetizing and applicable to today's cook. Detailed instructions for preparing "veal head in tomato sauce," or "peacock stew" may be looked for elsewhere, because it's doubtful that such recipes would encourage you to read on. In short, obsolete, unusual (except for one traditional recipe in the soup chapter), or impractical recipes will not be found here.

It's true that for many years Polish cooks had little access to modern kitchen conveniences that we take for granted. Appliances such as microwave ovens, food processors, slow cookers, electric mixers, blenders, and toaster ovens had until recently been all but unheard of by Polish household cooks. Fortunately, the modern cooking age has finally arrived, but it will take quite a while to work its way to mothers and grandmothers who still rely on traditional labor-intensive methods.

I grew up on the outskirts of a small village in northeastern Poland, a few miles from the Russian border. Our small farm, with its barn and stockade fence, was like thousands of others scattered across the Polish countryside. We drew all of our water by hand from a deep outside well, and carried it to the house in buckets. We cooked on cast-iron grates and burners over a firebrick stove fueled with pine wood we cut and split ourselves. Baking and cooking in the oven of a wood-fired stove are much more difficult than in easily regulated gas or electric ovens, because constant temperatures are difficult to maintain with wood heat. Temperatures are high at first, then gradually drop. Some Polish cookbooks even take the gradual temperature drop into account when giving cooking times.

These recipes are simple, straightforward, tasty, and nourishing. And there are a lot more than pierogies and golombkies. Indeed, you're going to find recipes for what both the modern and old-time Poles are eating today. This is a true potpourri of dishes that have evolved over the last ten centuries, fashioned by many influences.

Available Ingredients

Until recently, grocery stores in Poland were not what they were in Chicago, Toronto, London, or Rome. You wouldn't find counters brimming with fresh vegetables, or 23 kinds of frozen fish. Supplies were limited, seasonal, and erratic.

Only a few years ago a Polish butcher might have offered fatback, pork ribs, and a few hanks of sausage. Or he could as easily have had nothing. It all depended. Even the famed canned hams were a myth to most Poles; they had historically been produced almost entirely for export. This is not to say there was no meat. Thousands of homes and mini-farms, even today, are surrounded by neat picket fences that keep chickens, hogs, sheep,

goats, geese, and an occasional milking cow from straying. Although locally raised meat is a little easier to come by in rural areas, for many families it's still a prized commodity, something to be savored during hard times or on special occasions. And when meat is served, it's often extended as a filling, made into patties or cooked with vegetables in a goulash. Leftover bits and pieces find their way into sausage and cold cuts, such as head cheese and scrapple. Bones are saved for soups. Nothing is wasted.

For vegetables, almost every home, even in larger towns, has a backyard garden of cabbage, potatoes, beets, carrots, onions, and cucumbers. Herbs are grown in window boxes, and dried for year-round use.

During spring and especially fall, mushrooms of all kinds sprout like manna throughout the forests. There, men, women, and children forage with a passion that can only be believed when witnessed. Mushrooms are pickled, boiled, fried, baked, stuffed, and dried, and make their way into dozens of Polish recipes.

Wild blueberries are harvested, as are strawberries, raspberries, cranberries, and miscellaneous fruit and nuts.

The Baltic Sea is a prime source for herring and ocean fish. Freshwater species, such as northern pike, yellow perch, trout, and carp, are caught in the country's numerous lakes, rivers, and streams.

Polish History

Poland's northern and southern boundaries are well-defined geographically and relatively easy to defend. The Baltic Sea is on the north, with the

Carpathian and Sudetes mountains to the south. Trouble has come persistently from the eastern and western borders, which have traditionally been minor topographic features, such as small rivers that flow northward to the Baltic, across a wide plain that straddles most of Europe. Over the last thousand years of Polish history, scores of armies—Mongols, Teutonic Knights, Turks, Swedes, Germans, Austrians, Prussians, and Russians—thundered across this flat corridor. Time and again Poland was conquered, occupied, partitioned, and reconquered.

But its troubled years were interspersed with times during which the Polish nobility built alliances with the royal courts of other European nations. Indeed, for a while, Poland was looked upon as *the* major power and seat of culture. And intermarriages of Polish aristocracy with French and Italian royalty brought foreign customs and cuisines into play.

Those times, however, were brief. During the eighteenth century, Austria, Prussia, and Russia conquered Poland and divided it among themselves. Although there was no official Polish state during the entire nineteenth century, the Poles never ceased struggling for their independence. They clung to their customs and ways, battered and challenged as they were by the conquerors.

After World War I, Poland's independence was at last regained, only to be snuffed out several decades later by the brutal Nazi regime. Hitler wanted to Germanize Poland. He planned to annihilate the Polish people and culture completely to make way for those of Germany.

Following World War II, Russia and Poland signed an agreement that actually shifted Poland's boundaries westward. In the east, Poland lost to Russia more than 69,000 square miles and 10 million people. To the west, Poland gained more than 38,000 square miles and 8 million people from Germany. Even after the mass migration following the boundary shift, many "half" Germans—still living where their German ancestors had dwelt for generations—discovered that they were living within the newly created Polish state instead of Germany.

Russian influence continued to rise thereafter. It peaked in the early 1950s, when Poland's policies became identical to those of its huge eastern neighbor, and continued in force until the dramatic crumbling of the Berlin Wall.

Due largely to its volatile history—a history of wars, partitions, and occupations—and somewhat due to the benign foreign influences of milder times, Polish cuisine contains subtle characteristics from the cookery of countries like France, Germany, Italy, Hungary, Russia, and many others.

Religion and Holidays

Most of the Polish people are Roman Catholic, and Polish Catholicism is conservative in the strictest sense. Fridays are still meatless for much of the population, even when meat is available. That, coupled with spartan Lenten fasts, necessitated the development of meatless dishes.

The Catholic faith also gives cause for many celebrations, such as Christmas and Easter feasts, and baptism and wedding gatherings, for which traditional meals have evolved.

Three holidays—Easter, Christmas, and New Year's—are especially noteworthy.

Easter in Poland

Easter is the happiest day of the year, when the Catholic Church celebrates the resurrection of Christ, and Poles cap their spartan 40-day Lenten fast with a joyous breakfast feast. Even the countryside reflects the bright and cheerful mood, with larks and other songbirds punctuating the cool mornings with their singing, and flowers of all kinds in bloom amidst lush vegetation.

Throughout Poland the week before Easter finds housewives busy with spring cleaning and preparing the many dishes that will grace Easter-morning tables.

Although traditions vary from North to South Poland, here's how my mother and father and many of their friends celebrated Easter.

After a Good Friday dinner of herring and boiled potatoes with parsley, my mother and the children would decorate hard-cooked eggs. Some of the eggs would be dyed in water in which yellow-onion skins, red-onion skins, or beet peelings had been boiled. Others would be covered with intricate designs using beeswax and bright-colored paints.

Saturday was a day to complete preparations for Sunday's breakfast. Our best white linen was placed on the table and decorated with boughs of pine cut in the forest. A half-dozen crystal decanters were arranged on one end of the table, full of sparkling liquors in home-tinted ambers, brilliant reds, and deep greens. These, plus as least one bottle of clear vodka and another of pale-yellow egg liquor, would provide many toasts to our guests throughout the festivities. Tall vases of pussy willows were placed near the table, while others stood empty, awaiting the tulips and hyacinths that would be picked early Easter morning.

My mother would then fill an Easter basket with hard-cooked eggs, salt and pepper, cold cuts, sausage, wheat bread, slices of *babka* and *mazurka*, and a small pascal lamb (the symbol of Jesus) made of butter. She would take the complete basket to church to be blessed. The rest of the prepared foods remained in the refrigerator or root cellar. They included platters of sliced roast beef, roast turkey, roast goose or chicken, roast veal, roast suckling pig, baked ham, fish, sauces, salads, cheesecake with raisins, white frosted babkas, and a variety of mazurkas.

Sunday, after early-morning Easter Mass, my mother would walk the children to the church altar to smell the beautiful flowers and listen to the chirping of canaries hidden in small cages within the altar's Easter foliage. Then home to the breakfast buffet—an open house for neighbors and relatives that lasted most of the day.

At the door my mother would greet our guests, offering wedges of hard-cooked egg and wishes of good health and happiness. Then everyone would share all of the blessed foods from the basket before the main buffet began. At our house most of the dishes were served chilled, except a clear borscht and a pot of sauerkraut with white sausage.

Easter Monday is a holiday mostly for children. It's a day when godparents bring presents of baskets of candy and fruit, toys or clothes to their godchildren. Youngsters all over Poland eagerly await this day.

The old tradition of Smingus Dyngus is also played out this day. This is when a surprising splash of water may await you at any turn, even in your own bed. Beware of overhead balconies or stairwells. Look out for boys in trees or on rooftops. Whatever the circumstance, the dousing with water is always followed by the cheerfully spoken phrase "Smingus Dyngus" or other words meaning Monday morning pouring water. It provides plenty of fun for youngsters, but worries meticulous housekeepers, stern adults, and even teenage girls.

How would you like to be dressed in your only new Easter outfit, leaving home early in the morning for a full day of visiting friends, only to have your brothers throw you into a washtub of cold water?

Now that I look back on it, sometimes Smingus Dyngus wasn't that much fun.

Foodwise, Easter Monday is a lazy kind of day. Pots of *bigos* simmer on stoves throughout the country, and leftovers are the rule.

Christmas

There's something about Christmas Eve in Poland that never fails to brighten the faces of even the grumpiest of all Poles. Its joyous, emotional dinner celebration unites separated families and renews friendships that are often strained by the trying conditions of everyday life. The same neighbors who squabble the rest of the year across picket fences, chasing each other's livestock, leaving each other's gate open, will break bread together at the Christmas table among hearty hugs and tears of joy.

Centuries ago feudal-estate masters suspended the feudal order on Christmas Eve by inviting their servants to sit with them at the same table. Today, Christmas has continued to be a time when love, friendship, and, most of all, forgiveness reign.

My mother used to say that no one holding a grudge can have a peaceful, happy Christmas. Indeed, in Poland, Christmas is a time when you make up with your enemies, and when you comfort the sick, the poor, and the lonely,

Each year, in a gesture symbolic of the Christmas spirit, my mother, like thousands of other housewives, sets an extra place at the Christmas Eve dinner table. She lights a lone candle in the window facing the street. The candle flickers through the darkness in the hopes that Christ, in the form of a stranger, will join the family for dinner. It may also serve as a beacon to help guide the spirit of any family member who could not travel the distance in person.

As a reminder of Christ's humble birthplace, a handful of fresh straw is placed beneath the traditional white-linen tablecloth. Before the meal begins, a prayer of thanks is said. Slim wafers or pieces of unleavened bread similar to communion hosts, impressed with biblical figures of Christ, angels, lambs, or Blessed Mary, are passed to each participant. Several wafers are then taken to the barn and fed to the family livestock, another reminder of the Bethlehem stable. Other blessed wafers have already been mailed to faraway relatives and friends.

Individuals unaware of Polish customs are often surprised to learn that no meat is served during Christmas Eve dinner. Christmas Eve is a time of strict fasting, the closing hours of a four-week period of penance called Advent.

Although dinner is meatless, it doesn't mean the meal isn't a bountiful feast. It begins with at least three different soups, including a meatless borscht, closely followed by three traditional fish entrées of which at least two are carp and pike. A seemingly endless array of appetizers, garnishes, and accompaniments, the fruits of several days' preparation, are then served between steaming platters of sauerkraut and meatless pierogies. There are pickled beets, pickled mushrooms, pickled herring, and fish in tomato sauce. There's Christmas babka and spicy oven-browned poppy seed rolls. It's a grand celebration, much in the tradition of earlier elaborate festivities, or *Wigilias*, that features twelve full courses of food and drink, representing the twelve apostles of Jesus.

After the meal, without even stopping to clear the leftovers from the dinner table, my family always moved into the living room. There the children trimmed a freshly cut pine tree with help from their grandparents. While we hung candy, fruit, nuts, and homemade ornaments on the tree, my mother would fasten strings of dangling, recently baked, sweet-smelling *paczki* to the ceiling,

Then every year, like magic, Santa Claus—who suspiciously resembled an absent, portly uncle—would arrive in a red coat and black boots, carrying a large sack slung over one shoulder. The sack was full of gifts for the children. But it wasn't that easy! We had to work for them. Our Santa would make us sing a song, recite a poem, say a prayer, or perform a dance before we could make off with our prizes. All the while the food remained on the dinner table, with continuous snacking throughout the evening until we went to bed or left for *Pasterka*, Midnight Mass.

To those who didn't attend Midnight Mass, Christmas Day brings church, and a late morning or early afternoon buffet for relatives and friends.

Not much cooking is done on Christmas Day. Instead, it's a peaceful time, a time to relax and nibble on cold turkey and smoked pork loin, ham, veal, meat loaf with hard-cooked eggs, bigos, vegetable salad, and clear borscht with dried mushroom *uszka*. It's an all-day open house, with neighbors dropping in on one another and snacking on tortes and cheesecakes.

During the afternoon, young people form groups and go caroling through the streets, dressed as kings, shepherds, or other biblical characters. If they sing in front of your house and you don't give them food or vodka, they might pull your sleigh five houses down, or remove your fence gate, all in good humor.

New Year's Eve

New Year's Eve in Poland is similar to New Year's Eve throughout much of the world. Dances held in restaurants, schools, and auditoriums feature plenty of good companionship, music, drink, and food. Appetizers, both hot and cold, are prepared and brought by partygoers who share their creations with everyone at their table. It's the biggest, wildest party in Poland.

The following day, though, has a tradition all its own: the *kulig*. Throughout the countryside, shaggy brown-maned plow horses are hitched to sleighs or wagons piled high with hay. Then off go the sturdy steeds, snorting, prancing into the dusk along snow-covered forest trails, with sleigh bells jingling in the crisp air. They pull their passengers to a place in the forest where a bonfire is started and sausage is roasted next to a simmering pot of bigos. Beer and vodka flow freely, and stories are told long into the night.

The Social Nature of the Poles

Perhaps because the average Pole is not as mobile as his western cousin, most Polish entertaining is done at home with relatives or close friends. As you have already read, at these intimate parties, meals play a central role. The Pole is a notorious nibbler and muncher. While playing cards, watching television, or simply engaging in conversation, he'll often forego the main meat to pick at a variety of side dishes developed especially for entertaining. These are served along with relishes: pickled herring, mushrooms, cucumbers, or peppers; thin-sliced smoked pork loin; cheese; rolls; rye bread and the inevitable pastries. It's one small platter after another throughout the evening, each chased with tea, soda, wine, beer, or vodka.

Many family cooks in Poland don't follow written recipes. Instead, they cook by "feel" and taste, adding so much of this and so much of that. Unfortunately, this method produces almost as many unaccomplished cooks as it does good ones. So, to begin with at least, I recommend that you stick to the traditional recipes. Later, feel free to experiment with them. If you like more salt, pepper, paprika, or sour cream, fine. But remember to keep accurate records so you can duplicate any variations you'd like to prepare again.

When you are with family and friends and sit down to a meal based on recipes from this book, you can also share some of the information about Polish history and customs. When you pass the pierogies, pass along some Polish tradition as well. ❧

When I was a child, I remember traveling by train once a year to visit my aunt in Steczyn for our annual family gathering. Each year my brothers and I made a contest of guessing what main dish my aunt would prepare for dinner.

It was a contest rarely decided until the following morning. And then it was only by hearsay because most of us found it impossible to stay hungry and awake through the marathon-like appetizer courses, and the many hours of socializing that always preceded dinner.

Every year, upon our arrival in late afternoon, out would come platter after platter of *zakaski*. These Polish appetizers were served cheerfully by my aunt and her daughters. There were many types of cold fish—herring, northern pike, trout, and carp—smoked, pickled, salted, and marinated in sour cream sauces. There were attractively arranged plates of sliced, cold-smoked pork loin, kielbasa, chicken, tongue, and other specialty meats. And no party was without the lettuce-lined trays of pig's feet and cooked fish served chilled in a flavorful gelatin aspic. Many other bite-size morsels were also provided. They included homemade crackers, cold and hot stuffed hard-cooked eggs and mushrooms, pickled onions and mushrooms, chunks of soft and hard cheeses, and slices of crisp fresh vegetables.

The ever-present *ogorek*, or dill pickle, was there,

APPETIZERS

too. It was sliced lengthwise, served in a dish next to pickled red sweet peppers or pimentos.

Round and round the table these appetizers went, a free-for-all limited only by what my aunt could find at market and by her fertile imagination. And when one plate was cleaned, another—with an entirely different snack—was brought in its place.

All the while conversation flowed freely, often aided by a generous supply of Polish *spiritus* or vodka. Thus, the hours passed and, little by little, we children succumbed to the constant nibbling until we could eat no more and our eyelids grew heavy.

Even among the older children who attempted to save room and energy for dinner, all hopes were dashed with the arrival of the *kanapki*, or canapés. These traditional Polish creations followed the initial rounds of appetizers as sure as the Russian guards relieve each other at the Lenin Building in Warsaw Square.

As mentioned earlier, Poles are notorious munchers, capable of holding a social event around a dish of cottage cheese sprinkled with chopped chives. To that end, canapés are a snacker's dream—a little of this, a little of that; some sour, some sweet, some vegetable, some meat.

Like the zakaski, canapés are prepared almost entirely without official rules. It can be said only that they're made with small squares or rounds of white, rye, or wheat bread. A variety of pâtés, sauces, dressings, and flavored butters are spread over the bite-size breads. Then they're topped with ingredients such as sardines, chopped herring, anchovies, sprats, hard-cooked-egg slices, cheeses, cold meats, pickled mushrooms, tomatoes, green onions, horseradish, pickled beets, and sliced vegetables. The list runs on and on. In short, canapés can be thought of as dainty sandwiches without the tops, often impaled by wooden picks for easy handling and serving.

They're usually served cold, but sometimes, when the mood strikes the host's fancy, they can be prepared and served hot. ⚜

Steak Tartare

Befsztyk Tatarski

Be sure the beef is very lean, as fat is not appetizing in tartare.

Makes 6 side-dish servings, or 12 appetizers

1 pound lean beef top round or sirloin
6 egg yolks
1 teaspoon onion powder
1 teaspoon salt
¼ teaspoon freshly ground black pepper
1 teaspoon vegetable oil
¼ cup chopped fresh chives

Using a grinder or food processor fitted with a metal blade, process beef until finely minced. Process a second time. Do not puree. In a medium bowl, combine beef, egg yolks, onion powder, salt, pepper, and oil. Cover with foil and refrigerate for at least 1 hour. Garnish with chives. Serve as a side dish or a spread with crackers, bread, or toast.

Canapés with Eggs

Kanapki z Jajkami

Keep hard-cooked eggs on hand for this quick-to-fix appetizer.

Makes 20 appetizers

3 tablespoons butter or margarine, at room temperature
20 thin slices French bread
¼ cup chopped fresh chives
Salt
4 hard-cooked eggs
Mayonnaise, page 64, or other mayonnaise
Ground sweet paprika

Spread butter or margarine on 1 side of each bread slice. Sprinkle with chives. Season with salt to taste. Cut ¼ inch off both ends of each egg. Carefully slice each egg crosswise into 5 equal slices. Place 1 egg slice on each buttered bread slice. Spoon mayonnaise into a pastry bag fitted with a medium fluted nozzle. Pipe mayonnaise onto egg slices. Garnish with paprika. Arrange on a platter.

Variation
Place bite-size pieces of sliced, peeled cucumber, smoked ham, or sausage on mayonnaise flowers.

Stuffed Swirls

Ptysie

A delicious dessert when filled with a sweet cream or pudding.

Makes about 25

1 cup water

½ cup butter or margarine plus 2 tablespoons butter

½ teaspoon salt

1 cup all-purpose flour

5 medium eggs

2 medium onions, minced

1 pound fresh mushrooms, minced

1 tablespoon sour cream

Preheat oven to 400°F (205°C). Grease and lightly flour a large baking sheet. Combine water, ½ cup butter, and salt in a medium saucepan. Bring to a boil over medium heat. Add flour all at once. Stir vigorously with a wooden spoon until smooth and dough forms a ball and leaves side of pan. Remove from heat. Add eggs, 1 at a time, stirring after each addition until smooth. Spoon dough into a large pastry bag fitted with a large fluted nozzle. Pipe dollops of dough, about 1 tablespoon each, onto prepared baking sheet, leaving room for spreading. Bake for 20 to 25 minutes, or until golden brown. Let cool.

Melt the 2 tablespoons butter in a large skillet. Add onions and mushrooms; sauté over medium-low heat until tender. Stir sour cream into onion mixture; let cool.

Preheat oven to 350°F (175°C). Cut baked pastry swirls in half horizontally. Using a spoon or small paring knife, remove any soft dough inside puffs, leaving a hollow shell or crust about ¼ to ⅜ inch thick. Spoon about 1 tablespoon of the sour cream mixture in bottom portion of each swirl. Replace top portion of swirls. Bake on a large ungreased baking sheet for 10 minutes, or until heated through. ❧

Torte Canapés

Tort Kanapkowy

Firm, heavy loaves of bakery bread work best for this recipe.

Makes 16 to 20 appetizers

Meat Spread

½ cup ground cooked chicken, pork, veal, or beef

2 tablespoons butter or margarine

Green Spread

2 tablespoons chopped fresh parsley or chives

1½ tablespoons butter or margarine

1 tablespoon lemon juice

Pinch salt

Herring Spread

2 hard-cooked eggs, chopped

1 fillet herring in oil, drained and chopped

Tomato Spread

1 (3-ounce) package cream cheese, at room temperature

2 teaspoons tomato paste

1 garlic clove, crushed

Pinch salt

Onion Spread

½ medium onion, chopped

1 dill pickle, chopped

1 tablespoon sour cream

1 tablespoon shredded sharp Cheddar cheese

Several drops red food coloring or ¼ teaspoon beet juice

1 unsliced loaf Polish or German rye bread

Prepare spreads: Using a blender or food processor fitted with a metal blade, separately process the ingredients for each spread into a smooth paste.

Slice off ends and trim top, bottom, and side crusts of bread as needed. Cut trimmed bread into 6 (½-inch-thick) horizontal slices. Remove top bread slice from stack; set aside. Place a thin layer of each spread on the 5 remaining bread slices. Stack bread layers in their original positions. Top with remaining slice, then gently press layers together. Cut stacked loaf into serving-size squares or triangles. ❖

Stuffed Egg Shells

Jaja Faszerowane

For Easter, use decorated eggs to prepare these unique appetizers. Provide spoons for guests to scoop out the eggs from the shells.

Makes 6 appetizers

3 hard-cooked eggs, unpeeled

2 tablespoons sour cream

2 tablespoons dry bread crumbs

1 tablespoon chopped green onion

Salt

Freshly ground black pepper

2 tablespoons butter or margarine

Fold a cloth towel in several layers. Holding the towel in 1 hand, place 1 unpeeled egg on towel. Hold egg lengthwise. With a heavy, sharp knife, split egg lengthwise halfway through with a firm stroke of the knife. Firmly cut the rest of the way through so shell does not break apart. Repeat with remaining eggs. Carefully remove egg whites and yolks from shells. Reserve shells intact.

In a small bowl, chop egg whites and yolks together. Stir in sour cream, 1 tablespoon bread crumbs, and green onion. Season to taste with salt and pepper. Carefully pack equal amounts of egg mixture into each egg shell. Place remaining bread crumbs on a small plate. Dip flat surface of each stuffed egg shell in bread crumbs. Lightly press bread crumbs into egg mixture.

Melt butter in a medium skillet. Place stuffed egg shells, flat side down, in skillet. Cook over medium heat until lightly browned, 2 to 3 minutes. Serve immediately.

Make sure your guests don't eat the shells!⊰

Ham and Egg Wraps

Jaja Zawijane w Szynce

For a fast appetizer, serve these simple, tasty treats.

Makes 12 appetizers

3 hard-cooked eggs

12 (5 × 1-inch) thin slices ham

Small cooked or pickled onions

Red bell pepper slices, chives, or anchovies

Peel and quarter eggs. Wrap a ham slice around each egg quarter, leaving egg ends showing. Secure ham with a wooden pick. Garnish with onions and pepper slices.⊰

Egg Spread

Pasta z Jaj

A tasty spread, it's great for stuffing cucumbers or tomatoes.

Makes about 1½ cups

    4 hard-cooked eggs
    ⅓ pound thinly sliced baked ham
    2 tablespoons vegetable oil
    Ground sweet paprika
    Salt

Peel and quarter eggs. In a grinder or food processor fitted with a metal blade, process eggs and ham until finely ground. Do not puree. In a small bowl, combine eggs, ham, oil, and paprika. Season to taste with salt. ❧

Mushroom Rounds

Paszteciki z Pieczarkami

Serve these delicious hot appetizers for any occasion.

Makes 16 appetizers

Dough 1
    ⅔ cup all-purpose flour
    1 egg yolk
    2 tablespoons sour cream
    ¼ cup water
Dough 2
    ⅔ cup all-purpose flour
    ½ cup plus 1 tablespoon butter or margarine, at room temperature

    1 egg white, lightly beaten
    1 egg yolk, lightly beaten
    2 tablespoons butter or margarine
    ½ pound fresh mushrooms, minced
    3 tablespoons half-and-half
    ¼ teaspoon all-purpose flour
    ⅛ teaspoon salt
    Pinch freshly ground black pepper

For Dough 1: In a medium bowl, combine flour, egg yolk, sour cream, and water. Work into a soft, elastic dough. Knead 15 to 20 minutes. Cover; set aside.

For Dough 2: In a medium bowl, combine flour and butter into a smooth, soft dough. Divide dough into 3 balls. Cover dough balls; set aside.

On a lightly floured board, roll out Dough 1 into a rectangle about ¼ inch thick. Place 1 ball of Dough 2 on center of rolled dough rectangle. Gently press dough ball with your hands or rolling pin until dough ball is ¼ inch thick and covers a circular portion of Dough 1. Fold up both short sides of Dough 1 over rolled Dough 2 so ends meet in center. Reroll resulting dough combination into a rectangle ¼ inch thick. Repeat with remaining 2 balls of Dough 2. Roll dough jelly-roll style. Wrap dough in foil; refrigerate overnight.

Preheat oven to 400°F (205°C). Grease a baking sheet. Halve dough crosswise. On a lightly floured board, roll out half of dough into a rectangle ¼ to ⅜ inch thick. Using a round 2-inch cutter, cut dough rounds. Arrange 16 rounds on greased baking sheet, allowing room for spreading. Press leftover dough scraps into a ball. Roll to same thickness; cut as many dough rounds as possible. Repeat process with remaining dough until a total of 48 rounds are cut. With a 1-inch round cutter, cut out centers of 32 dough rounds not on baking sheets, forming doughnut shapes. Using a pastry brush, apply beaten egg white to top surface of 1 uncut dough round on baking sheet. Carefully position 1 doughnut cutout directly on top of brushed dough round. Lightly press doughnut cutout down with your fingertips. Brush egg white on top of doughnut cutout. Place a sec-ond doughnut cutout on top of the first, Pat lightly with your fingertips. Repeat process until all dough rounds on baking sheet have 2 doughnut cutouts "glued" on. Brush beaten egg yolk on top of doughnut cutouts.

Bake for 15 minutes, or until golden; let cool.

Melt butter or margarine in a small skillet. Add mushrooms; sauté until nearly tender. In a small bowl, combine half-and-half, flour, salt, and pepper; stir mixture into mushrooms. Simmer for 5 minutes. Set aside to cool. Fill each dough round with about 1 teaspoon cooled mushroom mixture. Bake for 8 to 10 minutes, or until hot. Serve immediately. ❖

Pickled Mushrooms

Marynowane Pieczarki

For best results, use small button mushrooms for this delightful appetizer.

Makes 2 pints

3 cups water

2 tablespoons salt

2 pounds fresh mushrooms, stems removed

Marinade

1¼ cups white vinegar

10 black peppercorns

2 bay leaves

In a large saucepan, combine water and salt; bring to a boil. Add mushrooms. Cover tightly and simmer over low heat for 10 minutes. Strain mushrooms; discard cooking liquid. Let cool.

Prepare Marinade: Simmer vinegar, peppercorns, and bay leaves in a small covered saucepan for 10 minutes over medium-low heat. Bring to a boil over medium heat.

Arrange equal amounts of mushrooms in 2 (1-pint) canning jars. Pour boiling marinade over mushrooms to cover. Place lids on jars; seal tightly. Let cool to room temperature; refrigerate overnight. Serve chilled.❧

Stuffed Mushrooms

Pieczarki Nadziewane

Poles say "Caps off" to this favorite appetizer.

Makes 20 appetizers

20 (1½- to 2-inch) fresh mushrooms (about 1 pound)

2 tablespoons butter or margarine

1 small onion, minced

3 tablespoons dry bread crumbs

1 tablespoon sour cream

1 hard-cooked egg, minced

1 egg, lightly beaten

1 tablespoon chopped fresh parsley

¼ teaspoon salt

⅛ teaspoon freshly ground black pepper

20 (1-inch) squares thinly sliced Gouda or Swiss cheese

Preheat oven to 400°F (205°C). Grease a 9- or 10-inch-square baking dish. Separate mushroom stems and caps; set caps aside. Finely chop stem pieces.

Melt butter in a small skillet over medium heat. Add onion; sauté until soft, about 3 minutes. In a small bowl, combine onion, chopped mushroom stems, bread crumbs, sour cream, and hard-cooked egg. Stir beaten egg into onion mixture. Stir in parsley, salt, and pepper until blended.

Pack about 1 rounded teaspoon stuffing mixture into each reserved mushroom cap. Arrange, stuffing side up, in greased dish. Place 1 cheese square on each cap. Bake, uncovered, for 20 to 25 minutes, or until mushrooms are cooked.❖

Toast with Sprats

Grzanki z Szprotka

Sprats are small fish, similar to sardines, canned and packed in oil. They are available at stores specializing in European food products.

Makes 24 appetizers

½ pound canned smoked sprats

¼ cup milk

1 soft dinner roll

2 tablespoons sour cream

1 tablespoon lemon juice

¼ teaspoon salt

⅛ teaspoon freshly ground black pepper

6 slices white or rye bread

6 thin slices mozzarella cheese

2 tablespoons butter or margarine, at room temperature

Chopped fresh parsley

Preheat oven to 450°F (230°C). Remove sprats from oil; drain well. Clean sprats by gently pulling off tails and backbones. In a small bowl, mash sprats with a fork.

Place milk in a shallow bowl. Break roll into pieces; soak roll pieces in milk. Combine roll and sprats with a fork. Stir in sour cream and lemon juice. Season with salt and pepper.

Trim off bread crusts. Cut each bread slice into 4 triangles. Diagonally cut each cheese slice into triangles. Spread butter on both sides of each bread slice. Arrange bread slices on a baking sheet. Evenly spread about 1 teaspoon sprat mixture on each bread slice. Top each with a piece of cheese. Sprinkle parsley over cheese. Bake for 4 to 5 minutes, or until lightly browned. Serve hot.❖

Meat Pâté

Pasztet

A popular pâté to serve on canapés, sandwiches, or other appetizers.

Makes 2 loaves

1 pound veal

¾ pound fatty pork from leg or shoulder

½ pound beef chuck

2 celery stalks

1 parsley root, halved

3 medium onions

4 medium carrots, halved

2 bay leaves

½ tablespoon dried marjoram

8 black peppercorns

7 dried mushrooms, soaked

1 pound beef liver

2 tablespoons fine dry bread crumbs

¾ cup milk

3 stale dinner rolls

3 eggs

1 teaspoon salt

¼ teaspoon freshly ground black pepper

¼ teaspoon ground nutmeg

8 crisp-cooked bacon slices

Lettuce leaves

Place veal, pork, beef, celery, parsley root, onions, carrots, bay leaves, marjoram, peppercorns, and mushrooms in a large pot. Add enough salted water to cover. Bring to a boil over high heat. Reduce heat to low. Simmer, partially covered, for 1½ to 2 hours. Add beef liver. Simmer, partially covered, for 1 hour. Strain, reserving cooking juices. Discard celery, parsley root, onions, carrots, bay leaves, and peppercorns.

Preheat oven to 350°F (175°C). Grease 2 (8 × 4-inch) loaf pans. Sprinkle each greased pan with 1 tablespoon bread crumbs. Place milk in a shallow bowl. Break rolls into pieces; soak roll pieces in milk. Using a grinder, grind cooked veal, pork, beef, mushrooms, liver, and soaked rolls into a large bowl. Grind resulting mixture a second time. Add eggs, 1 teaspoon salt, pepper, and nutmeg; stir to blend. If mixture is not moist enough, add a little reserved cooking juices.

Arrange 4 crisp bacon slices on bottom of each greased pan. Place equal amounts of meat mixture in each pan. Bake for 40 to 50 minutes, or until mixture sets and sides of meat mixture pull away from pan sides. Remove from oven; cool. To serve, slice pâté in pans or turn out of pans to slice. Line a serving plate with lettuce leaves. Arrange pâté slices on lined serving plate. ❖

Crabmeat Spread

Pasta z Krabow

A thick dressing of your choice can be substituted for the mayonnaise.

Makes about 2½ cups

1 (8-ounce) package cream cheese, at room
temperature
½ pound cooked crabmeat, chopped and chilled
2 tablespoons mayonnaise
2 tablespoons Worcestershire sauce
¼ teaspoon salt
Several leaves fresh lettuce
Dash ground sweet paprika
Fresh bread, toast, or crackers

Place cream cheese and crabmeat in a medium bowl. With a fork, stir in mayonnaise, Worcestershire sauce, and salt. Place crabmeat mixture in a small bowl. Cover and refrigerate overnight.

Before serving, line a small serving dish with lettuce. Turn out spread into serving dish. Garnish with paprika and serve chilled with bread. ⁂

Warsaw Herring

Sledz po Warszawsku

Serve this attractive appetizer in a clear glass dish.

Makes 12 to 16 servings

2 pounds small salted dressed herring
½ cup cold milk
2 tablespoons prepared mustard
1 medium dill pickle, finely shredded
1 medium apple, peeled, finely shredded
1 medium onion, shredded
½ pickled sweet red pepper or pimiento, minced
¼ teaspoon freshly ground black pepper
2 medium onions, thinly sliced
1 cup olive oil
Pimiento strips for garnish

In a large bowl, place herring in enough cold water to cover. Soak for 6 to 8 hours, changing water three times. Bone herring; remove skin. Cut each herring lengthwise into 2 fillets. Place fillets in a narrow baking dish. Pour milk over herring. Let stand at room temperature for 1 hour, turning herring several times. Remove from milk; pat dry. Discard milk.

On a flat work surface, arrange fillets. Spread mustard evenly over tops of fillets. In a medium bowl, combine dill pickle, apple, shredded onion, red pepper, and black pepper. Spread equal amounts of pickle mixture on fillets. Roll filets, lengthwise, jelly-roll style. Secure with wooden picks. Place half of the onions on bottom of a medium glass or ceramic jar or crock. Add herring rolls. Top with remaining onions. Drizzle oil over onions and herring. Cover; refrigerate for 2 to 3 days.

To serve, arrange herring rolls on a plate or in a clear glass dish. Garnish with pimiento strips. Let stand for 1 hour at room temperature.

Variation
If using small herring, layer herring rolls in a serving dish. ❖

Marinated Herring
Marynowane Sledzie

A popular herring dish in Poland, often prepared for special occasions and meatless holidays.

Makes 12 to 16 servings

1 cup white vinegar

1 cup water

5 black peppercorns

5 allspice berries

2 bay leaves, crushed

2 large onions, thinly sliced

2 pounds fresh dressed herring

2 or 3 herring milt sacs

3 tablespoons olive oil

In a medium saucepan, combine vinegar, water, peppercorns, allspice, and bay leaves. Bring to a boil. Cook, uncovered, over medium heat for 5 minutes. Add onions; reduce heat and simmer for 3 minutes. Remove from heat; let cool.

Drain onions, reserving vinegar mixture. Cut herring into 1½- to 3-inch pieces. In a medium glass or ceramic jar, or crock with a tight-fitting lid, arrange one layer of herring. Top with a thin layer of onions. Repeat layering process until all herring and onions are used.

In a small bowl, crush milt sacs. Stir into reserved vinegar mixture. Pour vinegar mixture over herring. Drizzle oil over herring. Cover with a tight-fitting lid. Gently shake jar or crock to evenly distribute vinegar mixture and oil. Refrigerate for 3 to 4 days before serving. ❖

Onion Rolls

Cebulak

Great to serve with soup or salad, it can also be served as a hearty appetizer.

Makes 36 to 40 rolls

Onion Filling
    2 tablespoons butter or margarine
    4 large onions, minced (3 to 3½ cups)
    ½ teaspoon salt
    ¼ teaspoon freshly ground black pepper

    2 (¼-ounce) packages active dry yeast
    (2 tablespoons)
    ½ cup warm water (110°F, 45°C)
    1 teaspoon sugar
    ¾ cup warm milk
    2 tablespoons plus 3 cups all-purpose flour
    ¼ teaspoon salt
    ¼ teaspoon ground nutmeg
    1 egg

Prepare Onion Filling: Melt butter or margarine in a medium skillet. Add onions; sauté over medium heat until tender. Season with salt and pepper. Let cool.

In a small bowl, dissolve yeast in ¼ cup of the warm water. Stir in the 2 tablespoons flour, sugar, and milk. Let stand until foamy, 5 to 10 minutes. Place the 3 cups flour, salt, and nutmeg in a large bowl. In a small bowl, beat egg and the remaining ¼ cup water; stir into yeast mixture. Add mixture to dry ingredients. Stir or knead mixture into a pliable dough.

Turn out dough onto a lightly floured surface. Clean and grease bowl. Knead dough 8 to 10 minutes or until smooth and elastic. Place dough in greased bowl, turning to coat all sides. Cover with a damp cloth. Let rise in a warm place, free from drafts, until doubled in bulk, about 2 hours.

Grease 2 baking sheets. Divide dough into 4 parts. Roll out one part of dough on an unfloured work surface until ⅛ to ¼ inch thick. Using a round 4-inch cutter, cut out dough. Place 1 teaspoon Onion Filling on center of 1 dough round. Spread to within ½ inch of edge. Roll jelly-roll style. Place onion roll, seam side down, on greased baking sheet. With your fingers, sharply bend ends of onion roll together until they touch each other, like a fortune cookie. Pinch to seal. Repeat process with remaining dough and Onion Filling until baking sheet is filled, leaving enough space between rolls for rising. Cover with a cloth. Let rise in a warm place, free from drafts, until doubled in bulk, about 1 hour.

Preheat oven to 350°F (175°C). Bake for 20 to 25 minutes, or until golden brown. Serve warm. ❧

Ham Triangles

Grzanki z Szynka

A fast, snappy appetizer to serve hot at parties.

Makes 16 appetizers

¼ cup minced ham

2 tablespoons grated provolone or Gouda cheese

2 tablespoons sour cream

4 slices slightly stale bread

2 tablespoons butter or margarine, at room
temperature

Preheat oven to 450°F (230°C). In a small bowl, combine ham, cheese, and sour cream. Cut each bread slice into 4 triangles. Spread butter on both sides of bread triangles; arrange on a baking sheet. Spread ham mixture evenly on top of each bread triangle. Bake for 10 to 12 minutes, or until browned. Serve hot.

Chicken Pâté

Pasztet z Kury

A grinder will help give the correct consistency for this popular spread.

Makes 1 loaf

4 cups water

Salt

1 (2- to 2½-pound) chicken, cut up

¼ pound chicken livers

¼ pound fresh bacon, chopped

2 stale dinner rolls

2 eggs, beaten

½ teaspoon ground nutmeg

Freshly ground black pepper

Heat water and ½ teaspoon salt in a large deep skillet. Add chicken, livers, and bacon. Bring to a boil over medium-high heat. Cover with a tight-fitting lid. Reduce heat to medium-low. Cook until chicken is tender, 1 hour. Remove chicken, livers, and bacon from cooking liquid; let cool. Reserve cooking liquid.

Preheat oven to 350°F (175°C). Grease a 9 × 5-inch loaf pan. Remove bones and skin from chicken. Break rolls into pieces. Soak roll pieces in reserved cooking liquid until moistened; squeeze out excess juice. Grind chicken, livers, bacon, and soaked rolls into a large bowl. Grind resulting mixture a second time. Blend in eggs and nutmeg. Season with salt and pepper. Place chicken mixture in greased pan; pat smooth.

Bake, uncovered, for 1 hour, or until pâté is firm; let cool. Cover; refrigerate for 48 hours before slicing and serving. ❧

My grandmother used to boast that she could make a pot of soup every day for three consecutive months without ever preparing the same soup twice. Although we never challenged her to try it, we never had reason to doubt her either.

Soups are very important in the daily Polish diet. You'll find a variety in this chapter unlike those served regularly in the West. In addition to "conventional" soups, such as chicken, vegetable, and tomato, Poles love sour soups made with dill pickles or sauerkraut. Or sweet dessert-like soups created from a host of fresh and dried fruits. Other popular soups include Barley-Vegetable Soup; Borscht, a delectable combination of meat and beef flavors; the ever-present Fish Soup; and a variety of cream soups thickened with sour cream and roux.

SOUPS

Tripe Soup is a Polish specialty, the mere mention of which will practically bring tears of longing to any Pole. Thoughts of the flavorful soups made from dried and fresh mushrooms cause similar reactions. Czarnina or "Black" or "Duck Blood" Soup will bring back memories for any individuals native to Poland. Its reliance on duck or goose blood, however, is somewhat misleading. In truth, other more traditional ingredients such as beef broth, pork ribs, vegetables, and seasonings play dominant roles in this delicious recipe.

There's even one dish called Nothing Soup, so named because it's made with neither meat nor vegetables. It has a wonderful taste, similar to that of custard. Children and others with a sweet tooth love it.

The Polish cook frequently garnishes his or her creations with home-grown herbs and greens. Chopped fresh parsley, chives, and dill top the list.

Root vegetables play an important role in Polish stocks and soups. In addition to beets and carrots, two traditional roots are used that are relatively unknown to Western cooks. One is called *parsley root* or *turnip-rooted parsley*. It's a member of the parsley family that expends most of its energy developing a taproot similar to a white-skinned carrot or parsnip. For centuries, parsley root has been used as a flavoring agent by European cooks, especially German, Hungarian, and Polish. Its leaves are larger and softer than the common sprig parsley found in most stores throughout the West. When minced, the leaves make an excellent and attractive garnish.

The other is called *celery root, celeriac, knob,* or *turnip-rooted celery.* It's a strange-looking vegetable, much like a be-whiskered turnip. Its globular root mass is the size and shape of a large plum, with many gnarled warts and threadlike roots trailing from its bottom. It gains respectability when trimmed, and has a wonderful celery flavor.

In the West, parsley root and celery root are

available in some large produce departments and specialty or ethnic stores. They can be grown in almost any location with soil and weather suitable for carrots or parsnips.

When parsley root isn't available, substitute several bunches of common parsley. If the recipe calls for the root to be ground, mashed, or shredded, use parsnips. Although the resulting flavor will not be the same, it probably will be acceptable to all but the most demanding purists.

Celery root is the rarer of the two vegetables. If it isn't available, substitute three or four celery stalks. Parsnips can also be used here, if desired.

When meat is not desired, items such as plain and stuffed dumplings, noodles, barley, rice, or vegetables can help turn a simple broth or soup into nourishing vegetarian fare.

In recent years it has not been uncommon for a Polish family to partake of soup four times in one day—breakfast, lunch, dinner, and supper. Dinner *and* supper? The typical Pole eats somewhat less per meal than his Western counterpart. However, to make up the difference, Poles eat more often. Instead of three meals per day, the Polish love of food has demanded four. Soup plays an important role in all of them. ❧

Bean Soup

Zupa Fasalowa

Almost any kind or combination of dried beans can be used: navy, baby lima, pinto, or others. Be careful not to add salt because enough will usually be present from the cooked ham bone.

Makes 8 to 10 servings

2 cups dried great Northern beans

3½ quarts water

¼ cup butter or margarine

2 large carrots, diced

2 leeks, minced

2 celery stalks, diced

1 medium onion, chopped

Bone from ½ cooked ham, with some meat still on

1 bay leaf

1 tablespoon chopped fresh thyme leaves

1 tablespoon chopped fresh parsley

¼ tablespoon freshly ground black pepper

Rinse beans. Place beans in a large bowl and add enough water to cover by 2 inches. Soak beans overnight; drain. Discard soaking water. Place beans in a large saucepan and cover with the water. Bring to boil over medium-high heat. Reduce heat to low; cook, uncovered, so liquid simmers but does not boil. Skim accumulations of surface foam occasionally with a skimmer or ladle.

Melt butter in a large pot. Add carrots, leeks, celery, and onion; sauté over medium-high heat until browned—a tinge of browned vegetables will add pleasant flavors. Add beans and cooking water plus ham bone. Add the herbs and pepper. Reduce heat to low; simmer, partially covered, until beans are tender, about 2 hours. Remove ham bone; let cool. Cut usable meat from ham bone into small pieces, and return ham pieces to the soup. Simmer for 20 minutes. Serve hot.

Tomato Soup

Zupa Pomidora

Use only ripe tomatoes for this recipe or the results may be too sour for your taste.

Makes 8 to 10 servings

2 tablespoons butter or margarine

1 large onion, diced

2 celery stalks, diced

2 large carrots, diced

1 tablespoon fresh thyme leaves

1 garlic clove, crushed

5 pounds ripe tomatoes, peeled and quartered

6 cups Beef Broth, page 341

Salt, to taste

¼ teaspoon freshly ground black pepper

1 bay leaf

1 teaspoon sugar

2 tablespoons grated Parmesan cheese, for garnish (optional)

Lazy Noodles, page 91 (optional)

Plain yogurt, for garnish (optional)

Melt butter in a large pot over low heat. Add onion, celery, and carrots; cook until vegetables are tender, 10 minutes. Stir in thyme and garlic. Cook 2 minutes. Add tomatoes, broth, salt, pepper, bay leaf, and sugar. Bring to a boil. Cook, partially covered, over medium-low heat, until tomatoes fall apart, 45 minutes.

Remove bay leaf. Let cool. Puree entire amount of soup in a blender or food processor.

Return processed soup to large pot. If a thinner soup is desired, add a small amount of water. Cook, uncovered, over medium-low heat for 20 minutes. Serve hot sprinkled with Parmesan cheese, with noodles, or with a dollop of plain yogurt in each serving (if using).

Black Soup

Czarnina

Sometimes called duck blood soup, this is a very simple, old-fashioned soup rarely found in modern cookbooks anymore because of the difficulty in obtaining fresh amounts—no matter how small—of duck or goose blood.

Makes 4 to 6 servings

Lazy Noodles, page 91

2 pounds pork ribs

5 cups water

1 large onion

2 large carrots, thinly sliced

3 celery stalks, thinly sliced

1 tablespoon chopped fresh parsley

1 cup fresh blood from duck or goose

1 cup dried prunes, soaked overnight in water to cover and cooked in soaking water until soft

2 apples

1 teaspoon sugar

½ teaspoon ground cinnamon

¼ teaspoon ground marjoram

¼ teaspoon freshly ground black pepper

½ teaspoon salt

Prepare noodle dough.

To a large pot, add pork ribs, water, onion, carrots, celery, and parsley. Bring to a boil over medium-high heat. Reduce heat to medium-low and simmer, covered, for 2 hours.

Strain broth into a large pot, discarding meat and vegetables; stir blood into broth. Add prunes with their cooking juice. Peel, core, and finely chop apples; add to broth. Add 1 teaspoon sugar, spices, and salt. Bring soup to a boil over medium-high heat. Boil 1 minute. Reduce heat to low. Simmer 10 minutes.

Cook noodles and drain. Serve hot soup over noodles.

Refreshing Strawberry Soup

Zupa Truskawkowa

For a Polish fruit drink on a hot summer day, chill this sweet soup.

Makes 4 servings

1 quart fresh strawberries

1¾ cups water

2 tablespoons sugar

1 tablespoon lemon juice

1 cup half-and-half

1½ cups cooked egg noodles (optional)

Reserve 4 whole strawberries; slice remaining strawberries. Place sliced strawberries and water in a medium saucepan. Bring to a boil over medium heat. Simmer, uncovered, over low heat for 30 minutes. Puree in a blender or food processor fitted with a metal blade.

Pour mixture back into medium saucepan. Stir in sugar and lemon juice. Add half and half. Simmer over low heat about 5 minutes; do not boil. Serve hot over noodles (optional), or serve chilled. Garnish with reserved whole strawberries. ❖

Cherry Soup
Zupa Wisniowa

Children love this soup.

Makes 6 servings

4 cups pitted dark sweet cherries
1 pint water (2 cups)
Lemon juice
3 tablespoons sugar
1 pint whipping cream (2 cups)
3 cups cooked egg noodles (optional)

In a large saucepan, combine cherries and water. Bring to a boil over medium heat. Puree cherries and water in a blender or food processor fitted with a metal blade. Return mixture to saucepan. Add lemon juice to taste, sugar, and whipping cream. Gently stir until smooth. Serve hot over noodles (if using), or serve chilled.

Variation
Substitute red tart cherries for sweet cherries. Do not add lemon juice. Sweeten with sugar to taste. ❖

Nothing Soup
Zupa Nic

This is one of the few soups you can prepare for dessert.

Makes 4 servings

3 eggs, separated
¾ cup sugar
5 cups milk
1 tablespoon Vanilla Sugar, page 174
Pinch salt
Ground cinnamon

In a medium bowl, beat egg whites until stiff but not dry. Fold in ¼ cup of the sugar. In a medium saucepan, combine milk and Vanilla Sugar. Bring to a boil over medium heat. Add 1 teaspoon of the egg-white mixture. When milk mixture comes to a boil again and egg white becomes like a dumpling, add another teaspoon of the egg-white mixture, Wait several seconds. Gently stir, turning egg-white dumplings over. Repeat with remaining egg-white mixture. When all dumplings are cooked, remove dumplings with a slotted spoon; place equal amounts in 4 serving bowls.

Remove milk mixture from heat. In a medium bowl, beat egg yolks and the remaining ½ cup sugar with an electric mixer until pale and creamy, 5 to 7 minutes. Fold into milk mixture; simmer over low heat for 5 minutes, stirring frequently. Add salt. Ladle milk mixture over dumplings. Lightly sprinkle with cinnamon. Serve hot or chilled. ❧

Meat Broth
Wywar Miesny

A basic, nourishing broth used in countless soups, sauces, and in main dishes.

Makes about 5 quarts

8 quarts water

8 to 9 pounds meaty bones and meat scraps from beef, pork, and veal, or a combination

2 medium onions, char-burned, see page 34

2 parsley roots, quartered

4 medium carrots, quartered

4 celery stalks, quartered

2 leeks

20 black peppercorns

2 tablespoons salt

Place water, bones, and meat in a large stockpot. Cover; bring to a boil. Skim foam from surface until surface is clear. Reduce heat to medium. Cook, uncovered, for 1 hour. Add onions, parsley roots, carrots, celery, leeks, peppercorns, and salt. Cover; bring to a boil.

Reduce heat to very low. Cover and simmer for 3 hours. Strain broth into a large bowl. Discard meat scraps, bones, and cooked vegetables. Cool broth, uncovered. Pour into quart or pint containers with tight-fitting lids. Refrigerate until fat congeals. Lift fat off with a fork; discard fat. Cover; refrigerate for up to 2 days or freeze for up to 3 months. Bring broth to a full boil before using.

Tip
To char-burn an onion using a gas stove, hold peeled onion over the open flame using metal tongs until slightly charred. With an electric stove, place onions under the broiler or halve them and burn the flat sides in an old frying pan. ❖

Beef Broth
Wywar Wolowy

Scraps of chicken and veal can be substituted for the beef.

Makes about 2½ quarts

4½ quarts water

3½ to 4 pounds meaty bones and beef scraps

1 large onion, char-burned, see Tip, page 34

2 medium carrots, cut in 2-inch pieces

1 parsley root, quartered

1 leek

1 celery root, quartered

½ head Savoy cabbage, quartered

12 black peppercorns

Salt

Place water, bones, and beef scraps in a stockpot. Bring to a boil over medium-high heat. Skim foam from surface until surface is clear. Reduce heat to medium. Cook, uncovered, for 30 minutes.

Add onion, carrots, parsley root, leek, celery root, cabbage, and peppercorns. Reduce heat to low. Partially cover; simmer for 2 to 2½ hours. Season with salt to taste. Strain broth into a large bowl. Discard beef scraps, bones, and cooked vegetables. Cool broth, uncovered. Pour into quart or pint containers with tight-fitting lids. Refrigerate until fat congeals. Lift fat off with a fork; discard fat. Cover; refrigerate for up to 2 days or freeze for up to 3 months. Bring broth to a full boil before using. ❖

Chicken Broth

Wywar z Kury

Excellent alone or as a light, richly flavored base for other soups.

Makes about 2 quarts

1 (3½-pound) chicken, cut up

About 3 quarts water

3 large onions, halved

1 large onion, char-burned, see Tip, page 34

1 leek

1 celery root, halved

1 parsley root, halved

1 head Savoy cabbage, quartered

4 allspice berries

2 teaspoons salt

8 black peppercorns

Place chicken and enough water to cover in a stockpot. Bring to a boil over high heat. Skim foam from surface until surface is clear. Reduce heat to medium-low; add remaining ingredients.

Simmer, partially covered, for 2 to 2½ hours. Strain broth into a large bowl. Discard cooked vegetables. Remove chicken meat from bones; reserve for other use. Discard bones and skin. Cool broth, uncovered. Pour into quart or pint containers with tight-fitting lids. Refrigerate until fat congeals. Lift fat off with a fork; discard fat. Cover; refrigerate for up to 2 days or freeze for up to 3 months. Bring broth to a full boil before using.

Vegetable Broth

Wywar z Warzyw

This light, nourishing broth is served frequently during religious holidays.

Makes about 2½ quarts

2 tablespoons butter or margarine

2 medium onions, chopped

4 quarts water

3 medium carrots, sliced

2 parsley roots, sliced

2 celery roots, sliced

1 leek

2 small celery stalks including leaves

½ head Savoy cabbage, quartered

2 tablespoons chopped fresh dill, or 1 tablespoon dill weed

15 black peppercorns

Salt

Melt butter in a medium skillet. Add onions; sauté over medium heat until tender. In a large stockpot, combine onions, water, carrots, parsley roots, celery roots, leek, celery, and cabbage. Bring to a boil over high heat. Reduce heat to low. Add dill and peppercorns.

Partially cover; simmer for 1 to 1½ hours. Strain broth into a large bowl. Season with salt to taste. Discard cooked vegetables. Cool broth, uncovered. Pour into quart or pint containers with tight-fitting lids. Refrigerate for up to 2 days or freeze for up to 3 months. Bring broth to a full boil before using.

Tip
Fat removed from poultry and other meat broth can be used as a flavorful fat for frying or sautéing meat. ❖

Veal Broth
Wywar z Cieleciny

For maximum flavor, ask your butcher to cut veal bones in half to expose the marrow.

Makes about 2 quarts

3½ to 4 pounds meaty veal bones

2½ quarts water

1 parsley root, halved

2 leeks

1 celery root, halved

4 medium carrots, halved

1 medium onion

½ pound green cabbage

8 black peppercorns

In a large stockpot, boil enough water to cover veal bones. Add veal bones; bring water back to a boil. Drain; discard water. Add the 2½ quarts water. Cover; bring to a boil over medium heat. Skim foam from surface until sur-face is clear. Cook for 30 minutes. Add parsley root, leeks, celery root, carrots, onion, cabbage, and peppercorns. Bring mixture to a boil.

Reduce heat and cover. Simmer for 1½ hours. Simmer, uncovered, for 10 minutes. Strain broth into a large bowl; reserve veal for other use. Discard cooked vegetables. Cool broth, uncovered. Pour into quart or pint containers with tight-fitting lids. Refrigerate until fat congeals. Lift fat off with a fork; discard fat. Cover, refrigerate for up to 2 days or freeze for up to 3 months. Bring broth to a full boil before using. ❖

Dried Mushroom Soup

Barszcz Grzybowy

For a meatless Christmas Eve soup, substitute water for meat broth.

Makes 6 to 8 servings

3 cups water

2 ounces dried mushrooms

2 quarts Meat Broth, page 33, or bouillon

3 tablespoons butter or margarine

1 leek, minced

1 large carrot, grated

1 medium celery root, grated

2 medium onions, chopped

1 tablespoon vegetable oil

1 tablespoon all-purpose flour

Salt

Freshly ground black pepper

Polish Ravioli, page 103 (optional)

Chopped fresh parsley or dill

In a medium saucepan, bring water to a boil. Cool slightly. Add mushrooms; cover with a tight-fitting lid and refrigerate overnight. Bring mushrooms to a boil, uncovered, over high heat. Reduce heat to low. Simmer for 1 hour. Remove mushrooms from liquid and cool; reserve liquid. Chop mushrooms; return to reserved liquid.

Heat broth in a large saucepan. Melt butter in a large skillet over medium-low heat. Add leek, carrot, celery root, and onions. Sauté until tender, 10 to 15 minutes. Add sautéed vegetables to hot broth. Simmer, partially covered, over low heat for 1 hour. Strain liquid; discard vegetables. Add mushrooms and mushroom liquid to strained liquid. Bring to a boil over medium heat.

Heat oil in a small skillet over medium heat. Stir in flour; cook, stirring, until golden. Ladle 1 cup of the broth from soup into flour mixture. Stir to combine. Return resulting mixture to soup. Bring to a boil, stirring constantly. Season with salt and pepper to taste. Serve hot, over ravioli (if using). Garnish with parsley. ❧

Fresh Mushroom Soup

Zupa Pieczarkowa

Each variety of edible mushroom lends its own unique flavor to this soup.

Makes 4 servings

2 tablespoons butter or margarine

1 pound fresh mushrooms, thinly sliced

1 quart Meat Broth, page 33, or bouillon

1 tablespoon Maggi seasoning

1 teaspoon sugar

Salt

Ground white pepper

1 tablespoon all-purpose flour

¾ cup sour cream

Chopped fresh parsley

Melt butter in a large skillet over medium heat. Add mushrooms; sauté until tender. Heat broth in a medium saucepan; add mushrooms. Bring to a boil. Cover with a tight-fitting lid; simmer over low heat for 15 minutes. Add Maggi seasoning and sugar. Season with salt and white pepper to taste.

In a small bowl, combine flour and sour cream until smooth. Stir 1 cup of the hot broth into sour cream mixture until smooth. Add sour cream mixture to soup. Bring to a simmer, stirring constantly; do not boil. Ladle steaming soup into serving bowls. Garnish with parsley.

Onion Soup

Zupa Cebulowa

For flavor variations, substitute Gouda or other cheeses for the mozzarella.

Makes 8 servings

Cheese Grzanki

   8 slices slightly stale French bread

   2 tablespoons butter or margarine, at room temperature

   Grated Parmesan cheese

   Ground sweet paprika

2 pounds onions (about 10 medium onions)

3 tablespoons butter or margarine

2 quarts Veal Broth, page 36, or bouillon

Salt

¼ cup white wine

Sugar

8 thin slices mozzarella cheese

Ground sweet paprika

Prepare Cheese Grzanki: Preheat oven broiler. Butter both sides of bread slices; arrange on a baking sheet. Sprinkle Parmesan cheese and paprika over bread slices. Broil for 3 to 5 minutes, or until golden brown. Set aside.

Halve onions lengthwise, then slice thinly. Melt butter in a large skillet over medium heat. Add onions; sauté until onions turn a light golden color, 15 minutes. Heat broth in a large saucepan. Add onions. Season with salt to taste.

Bring to a boil. Reduce heat to low. Simmer for 30 minutes, uncovered. Add wine and sugar to taste if onions are not sweet enough.

Preheat broiler. Ladle soup into 8 ovenproof serving bowls. Place 1 Cheese Grzanki on top of soup in each bowl. Top each Cheese Grzanki with 1 slice cheese. Sprinkle cheese with paprika. Place filled serving bowls under broiler. Broil for 5 minutes, or until cheese melts and begins to brown. ⁂

Potato Soup

Zupa Ziemniaczana

For variety, use chicken, veal, beef, or pork broth.

Makes 6 to 8 servings

6 medium potatoes, peeled, cut into ½-inch cubes
2 medium carrots, thinly sliced
2 celery stalks, thinly sliced
1 medium onion, chopped
1½ quarts water
2 cups Meat Broth, page 33, or bouillon
2 tablespoons butter or margarine
2 tablespoons all-purpose flour
½ teaspoon salt
¼ teaspoon ground white pepper
1 cup milk
Chopped fresh parsley

Place potatoes, carrots, celery, and onion in a large saucepan. Add water and broth. Cover with a tight-fitting lid. Cook over medium heat until vegetables are tender, 30 minutes.

Melt butter in a small saucepan over medium heat. Stir in flour, salt, and white pepper. Cook, stirring constantly, until mixture bubbles. Slowly add ¼ cup of the milk; cook, stirring, until smooth. Add remaining milk, stirring until smooth. Bring to a boil, stirring constantly. Stir into hot broth mixture. Bring to a simmer over medium heat. Reduce heat to low and simmer for 10 minutes. Serve hot, garnished with parsley. ⁂

Barley-Vegetable Soup

Krupnik

This soup will take the chill out of winter evenings.

Makes 6 to 8 servings

¼ cup butter or margarine
1 medium carrot, sliced
1 leek, sliced
1 celery stalk, sliced
1 small onion, chopped
¼ cup barley grits
2 quarts Meat Broth, page 33, or bouillon
2 bay leaves
4 black peppercorns
1 teaspoon salt
4 large dried mushrooms
4 medium potatoes, peeled, diced
Chopped fresh parsley

Melt butter in a large skillet over medium heat. Add carrot, leek, celery, onion, and barley. Cook, uncovered, for 10 to 12 minutes, stirring several times.

In a large saucepan, bring broth to a boil. Add vegetables, bay leaves, peppercorns, and salt. Cover; bring to a boil. Reduce heat to low; cook for 30 minutes.

Wash and chop dried mushrooms. Add mushrooms and potatoes to broth mixture. Cover and simmer over low heat until potatoes are tender, 30 minutes. Remove and discard bay leaves. Ladle hot soup into serving bowls. Garnish with parsley. ❧

Kohlrabi Soup

Zupa z Kalarepy

Kohlrabi is not a cabbage or a turnip, yet in many ways resembles both.

Makes 8 to 10 servings

1½ quarts water
About 1 pound young kohlrabi, peeled, quartered
½ celery root, halved
1 parsley root, halved
2 leeks, white part only
2 tablespoons butter or margarine
1 tablespoon all-purpose flour
1 quart Meat Broth, page 33, or bouillon
2 egg yolks
1 cup half-and-half
Salt
Sugar
¼ cup chopped fresh dill
Cheese Grzanki, page 38 (optional)

Heat water in a large saucepan. Add kohlrabi, celery root, parsley root, and leeks. Cook, covered, over medium-low heat until vegetables are tender, 30 minutes. Strain stock into a large saucepan; discard celery root, parsley root, and leeks. Rub about half of the kohlrabi through a sieve into the stock. Discard remaining kohlrabi.

In a small skillet, melt 1 tablespoon of the butter. Add flour; cook over medium heat, stirring, until smooth. When flour mixture starts to bubble, stir in 1 cup of the broth. Stir thinned flour mixture into kohlrabi stock. Add the remaining broth. Bring to a boil. Remove from heat.

In a medium bowl, combine egg yolks and half-and-half. Pour egg yolk mixture into hot soup, stirring rapidly. Add the remaining 1 tablespoon butter. Season with salt and sugar to taste. Add dill and Cheese Grzanki (if using).

Cauliflower Soup
Zupa Kalafiorowa

Homemade String Noodles add just the right touch to this light and tangy soup.

Makes 6 servings

> String Noodles, page 91
> 1 medium cauliflower
> 1 pint water
> 2 quarts Veal Broth, page 36, or bouillon
> ½ pint sour cream (1 cup)
> 3 tablespoons all-purpose flour
> 1 teaspoon sugar
> Salt
> Chopped fresh parsley

Prepare String Noodles.

Wash cauliflower; separate into flowerets. Cut into 1-inch pieces. In a medium saucepan, place cauliflower and water. Cook over high heat, uncovered, until cauliflower is tender and water evaporates, 20 minutes.

In a large saucepan, bring broth to a boil. Add cauliflower. In a small bowl, combine sour cream and flour until smooth. Stir 1 cup of the hot broth into flour mixture. Stir resulting mixture into soup. Add sugar. Season with salt to taste. Place noodles in serving bowls. Ladle steaming soup over noodles. Garnish with parsley.

Variation

In a small bowl, combine ½ pint sour cream (1 cup) with 3 egg yolks, instead of flour. Gently stir into soup before serving. ❖

Dill Pickle Soup

Zupa Ogorkowa

This soup is a favorite with pregnant Polish women, and expectant fathers as well.

Makes 6 servings

2½ quarts water

2½ pounds pork spareribs

2 medium carrots, sliced

½ celery root

1 parsley root

1 bay leaf

10 black peppercorns

½ teaspoon salt

3 medium potatoes, peeled, quartered, sliced

2 tablespoons butter or margarine

4 medium dill pickles, peeled, grated

1 tablespoon all-purpose flour

½ cup sour cream

Dill pickle juice (optional)

Place water and spareribs in a large saucepan. Bring to a boil over medium-high heat. Skim foam from surface until surface is clear. Cook, uncovered, for 10 minutes. Add carrots, celery root, parsley root, bay leaf, peppercorns, and salt. Reduce heat to medium-low. Cook, uncovered, until meat is tender, 1 hour. Remove meat and bones; reserve for other use. Add potatoes; cook until tender, 20 minutes.

Melt butter in a small skillet over medium heat. Add pickles; sauté until tender, 8 to 10 minutes. Add to soup. Bring to a boil. Simmer, uncovered, over low heat for 45 minutes. Remove celery root, parsley root, and bay leaf; discard.

In a small bowl, combine flour and sour cream until smooth. Stir 1 cup of the broth into sour cream mixture until smooth. Return sour cream mixture to soup. Simmer for 5 minutes; do not boil. Serve hot. If soup is not sour enough, add dill pickle juice to taste. ❖

Fresh Dill Soup

Zupa Koperkowa

A classic Polish soup, it is excellent made with chicken, veal, or rabbit.

Makes 6 servings

String Noodles, page 91
2 quarts Meat Broth, page 33; Vegetable Broth, page 35; or bouillon
2 tablespoons butter or margarine
1 cup chopped fresh dill with no seeds or branches
Salt

Prepare noodle batter.

In a large saucepan, bring broth to a boil. Drizzle noodle batter into boiling liquid with a spoon, a few drops at a time, while stirring gently.

Melt butter in a small skillet over medium heat. Add dill; sauté until almost tender, 3 minutes. Do not brown. Stir dill into hot liquid. Simmer over low heat, covered, for 5 minutes. Season with salt to taste.

Variations
Instead of String Noodles, add ½ cup cooked long-grain white rice.

Potato-Dill Soup: In a small bowl, combine ¾ cup sour cream and 3 tablespoons all-purpose flour until smooth. Add 1 cup broth or bouillon; blend. Stir sour cream mixture into soup. Add about 2 cups diced, peeled, cooked small new potatoes.

Fresh Cabbage Soup

Zupa ze Swieżej Kapusty

Prepare this fast, inexpensive, tasty soup when time is at a premium.

Makes 6 servings

2 to 2¼ cups chopped green cabbage
1 medium onion, chopped
1 pint water
½ cup sour cream
1 tablespoon all-purpose flour
5 cups Chicken Broth, page 35; Veal Broth, page 36; Meat Broth, page 33; or bouillon
1 tablespoon Maggi seasoning
Salt
Pinch ground white pepper
Chopped fresh parsley or dill

Place cabbage, onion, and water in a medium saucepan. Cook, uncovered, over medium heat until tender, 15 to 20 minutes.

In a small bowl, combine sour cream and

flour until smooth. Bring broth to a boil in a large saucepan over medium heat.

Stir 1 cup of the hot broth into sour cream mixture. Return mixture to saucepan. Bring to a boil, uncovered, over medium-high heat, stirring occasionally. Add cabbage mixture. Simmer, uncovered, over low heat 10 minutes. Add Maggi seasoning. Season with salt and white pepper to taste. Simmer for 5 minutes. Serve steaming hot, garnished with parsley. ❖

Sauerkraut Soup

Kapusniak

For a milder flavor, rinse the sauerkraut before using it.

Makes 10 servings

- 1 pound sauerkraut
- 1 (2- to 2½-pound) ham bone
- 6 black peppercorns
- 1 bay leaf
- 3 quarts water
- 6 medium potatoes, peeled, diced
- ¼ pound bacon, diced
- 2 medium onions, chopped
- 2 tablespoons all-purpose flour

Place sauerkraut, ham bone, peppercorns, bay leaf, and water in a stockpot. Cover; bring to a boil. Uncover; cook over medium heat for 1½ hours.

In a medium saucepan, cook potatoes with enough water to cover until tender; drain well. Add potatoes to sauerkraut mixture.

In a small skillet, sauté bacon over medium heat until crisp. Remove bacon and drain on paper towels. Reserve 2 tablespoons bacon drippings in skillet. Add bacon to sauerkraut mixture. Add onions to reserved drippings; sauté onions, stirring, until golden brown. Stir in flour. Ladle 1 cup of the sauerkraut broth into onion mixture; stir to combine. Stir resulting mixture into soup. Bring to a boil. Remove and discard bay leaf. Serve hot.

Tip
After lending their unique flavors to broth, firm root vegetables, such as carrots, parsley root, and celery root, can be diced and included in mixed-vegetable side dishes. ❖

Cold Cucumber-Beet Soup

Chlodnik

This is a refreshing chilled soup; prepare it for lunch on hot summer days.

Makes 6 to 9 servings

1 pound small beets with greens (8 to 10 beets)
2 quarts Beef Broth, page 34, or bouillon
2 tablespoons lemon juice or vinegar
1 pint sour cream, sour milk, or buttermilk
(2 cups)
2 medium cucumbers, peeled, thinly sliced
6 radishes, thinly sliced
2 tablespoons chopped fresh dill or 1 tablespoon dried
1 tablespoon chopped fresh chives
1 teaspoon salt
3 hard-cooked eggs, thinly sliced or chopped

Scrub beets; rinse beet greens. Peel, then slice beets; chop beet greens. In a large saucepan, combine beets, greens, broth, and lemon juice. Cover with a tight-fitting lid. Bring to a boil over high heat. Reduce heat to low; simmer, partially covered, until tender, 30 minutes. Strain liquid into a large bowl; reserve beets and beet greens. Let strained liquid cool.

Add sour cream to cooled liquid; beat with an electric mixer until frothy, 2 to 3 minutes. Stir in beets, beet greens, cucumbers, radishes, dill, chives, and salt. Refrigerate for 1 hour. Serve chilled, garnished with eggs.

Variations
Add 1 cup chopped cooked veal.

Add 10 medium shrimp, shelled, deveined, cooked, and diced.

Add 2 thinly sliced dill pickles.

Borscht

Barszcz

This is one of the most traditional Polish soups.

Makes 6 servings

1½ pounds fresh beets
1 tablespoon salt
2 quarts Meat Broth, page 33; Beef Broth, page 34; or bouillon
2 tablespoons vinegar
Pinch freshly ground black pepper
Lemon juice
Sugar
Chopped fresh dill or parsley

Scrub and rinse beets clean; rinse with cold water. Leave roots, 1 to 2 inches stem, and skin intact. Place whole beets in a large saucepan, Add salt and enough cold water to cover. Bring to a boil over high heat. Cover with a tight-fitting lid; reduce heat to medium-low. Cook until tender, 1 hour. Remove beets from liquid. Let cool, then peel.

Heat broth in a large saucepan. Slice or grate beets; add to broth. Simmer, uncovered, over low heat for 30 minutes. Stir vinegar and pepper into beet mixture. Season with lemon juice and sugar to taste. Simmer over low heat for 1 hour; do not boil. Strain into a serving tureen. Serve steaming hot. Garnish with dill.

Variation
Christmas Eve Borscht: Substitute Vegetable Broth, page 35, for Meat Broth or bouillon. Add 1 tablespoon vegetable oil. Serve hot over Mushroom-Filled Ravioli, page 103.

Tripe Soup
Flaki

A favorite of native Poles, this soup is well worth the effort.

Makes about 6 servings

3½ pounds beef tripe

3 quarts water

2 carrots, whole

1 parsley root, whole

2 leeks, dark green leaves trimmed, cleaned

3 small onions

4 celery stalks

¼ cup butter or margarine

⅓ cup grated parsley root

½ cup grated carrot

1½ quarts Beef Broth, page 34, or bouillon

5 black peppercorns

½ teaspoon salt

⅛ teaspoon ground marjoram

⅛ teaspoon ground nutmeg

1 tablespoon Maggi seasoning

2 tablespoons all-purpose flour

Add tripe to a large stockpot; cover with water. Bring to a boil and boil for 5 minutes. Discard water. Rinse tripe with cold water. In same stockpot, place 3 quarts water, tripe, whole carrots, whole parsley root, 1 of the leeks, 2 of the onions, and 2 of the celery stalks. Cover; cook over medium heat for 3½ hours. Remove tripe; let cool. Discard cooking liquid and cooked vegetables.

Cut tripe, white part of the remaining leek and remaining celery stalks into thin strips, ¼ inch wide and 1 to 1½ inches long. Quarter and slice remaining onion into strips.

In a medium skillet, melt 2 tablespoons of the butter over medium heat. Add leek, onion, and celery. Add grated parsley root and grated carrot. Sauté over medium heat for about 5 minutes. Add ¼ cup water. Cover and cook over medium heat for 10 minutes, stirring several times.

Add broth, peppercorns, tripe, and cooked vegetables to a large saucepan. Bring to a boil. Reduce heat to low. Add salt, marjoram, nutmeg, and Maggi seasoning.

In a small skillet, melt the remaining 2 tablespoons butter over medium heat. Stir in flour; cook, stirring, until golden. Ladle 1 cup of the broth into flour mixture. Stir to combine. Return resulting mixture to soup. Bring soup to a boil. Serve hot. ❧

Fish Soup
Zupa Rybna

Most fresh-water fish can be used in this basic recipe.

Makes 4 to 6 servings

Fish Croquettes, page 147
2 pounds fresh fish, dressed
2 quarts water
2 medium carrots, quartered
2 medium onions
6 black peppercorns
1 bay leaf
3 allspice berries
Salt
Thin lemon slices

Prepare Fish Croquettes.

In a large stockpot, combine fish, water, carrots, onions, peppercorns, bay leaf, and allspice. Simmer, uncovered, over low heat until fish is easily removed from bones, 30 minutes. Strain into a large bowl. Reserve broth; discard solids. Add Fish Croquettes to broth. Season with salt to taste. Simmer over low heat for 5 minutes. Serve garnished with lemon slices. ❧

Beef-Cabbage Soup

Kapusniak Wolowy

Some Polish cooks like to brown the beef cubes just short of burning them, for a measure of extra flavor.

Makes 8 to 10 servings

> 2 tablespoons vegetable oil
> 1 pound boneless beef chuck roast, cut into
> 1-inch cubes
> 3 medium onions, sliced
> 1½ teaspoons salt
> 1½ quarts Beef Broth, page 34, or bouillon
> ½ medium head green cabbage, shredded
> 4 medium carrots, thinly sliced
> 2 tablespoons vinegar
> 1 tablespoon sugar
> 1 (28-ounce) can crushed tomatoes
> ½ teaspoon freshly ground black pepper

Heat oil in a large saucepan over medium-high heat. Add beef cubes and onions. Cook, stirring, until beef browns. Reduce heat to low. Add salt and broth. Cover and cook until beef cubes are tender, 1½ to 2 hours. Add cabbage and carrots. Cover and cook for 20 minutes. Stir in vinegar, sugar, and tomatoes. Season with pepper and heat until hot.

Farmer's Vegetable Soup

Gospodarska Zupa Warzywna

Use this delicious, nutritiously balanced soup as a main dish.

Makes 8 to 10 servings

> 2 quarts Meat Broth, page 33, or bouillon
> ⅓ cup cut fresh green beans
> ⅓ cup cut fresh yellow beans
> ½ celery root, diced
> ⅓ cup sliced carrot
> ⅓ cup ½-inch kohlrabi cubes
> ½ cup chopped green cabbage
> 2 parsley roots or 1 large bunch parsley sprigs tied together
> 2 bay leaves
> 10 black peppercorns
> 1 cup diced, peeled new potatoes
> ⅓ cup fresh or frozen green peas
> ½ cup fresh or frozen whole-kernel corn
> ½ pint sour cream (1 cup)
> 2 tablespoons all-purpose flour
> Salt

Heat broth in a stockpot. Add beans, celery root, carrot, kohlrabi, cabbage, parsley roots, bay leaves, and peppercorns. Partially cover; cook over medium-low heat for about 20 minutes. Add potatoes; cook over medium heat, partially covered, for 20 minutes. Add peas and corn; cook until vegetables are tender, 10 minutes.

In a medium bowl, combine sour cream and flour. Stir 1 cup of the hot broth into sour cream mixture until smooth. Return sour cream mixture to soup, stir to blend. Season with salt to taste. Remove and discard bay leaves and parsley sprig bunch, if used. Serve hot.

Yellow-Pea Soup

Grochowka

Smoked ham lends a distinctive flavor to this nourishing dish.

Makes 6 to 9 servings

Ham Broth
  2 to 2½ pounds smoked ham with bone
  3 celery stalks
  4 medium carrots, quartered
  1 parsley root
  1 leek
  10 black peppercorns
  1 bay leaf
  1 teaspoon salt
  3 quarts water

  1 cup dried yellow split peas
  1 quart water
  4 medium potatoes, peeled, diced
  2 ounces bacon, diced
  ¼ cup minced onion
  1 tablespoon all-purpose flour
  Chopped fresh parsley

Prepare Ham Broth: Place all ingredients in a stockpot. Cover with a tight-fitting lid. Simmer over low heat for 2½ hours. Strain; reserve ham for other use. Discard vegetables.

In a medium saucepan, combine split peas and water. Cover with a tight-fitting lid. Bring to a boil. Reduce heat to low; simmer until peas are tender, 2 hours. Drain peas in a fine-mesh metal strainer; discard liquid.

Pour Ham Broth into a large saucepan. Using the back of a wooden spoon, mash peas through strainer into broth. Ladle broth through strainer until only hulls remain in strainer. Add potatoes to broth. Bring to a boil. Cook over medium heat, uncovered, until potatoes are tender, 20 minutes.

In a small skillet, sauté bacon over medium heat until crisp. Add onion; sauté until tender. Stir flour into bacon and onion. Cook over medium heat, stirring, until flour becomes golden, 2 to 3 minutes. Ladle 1 cup of the broth into bacon mixture. Stir to blend in flour. Combine resulting mixture with soup. Bring to a boil. Serve hot, garnished with parsley.

Tomato Soup

Zupa Pomidorowa

Of all the Polish soups, this is my favorite.

Makes 8 to 10 servings

3 tablespoons butter or margarine
4 pounds fresh tomatoes, quartered (about
16 medium tomatoes) or 1 (6-ounce) can tomato
paste
2 quarts Chicken Broth, page 35; Meat Broth,
page 33; or bouillon
3 tablespoons all-purpose flour
½ pint sour cream (1 cup)
1 tablespoon sugar
Salt
Chopped fresh parsley or dill

Melt butter in a large skillet over medium heat. Add fresh tomatoes; cover and cook over medium heat, stirring occasionally, until skins shrivel, 20 minutes. Pour tomatoes into a fine-mesh strainer. With a wooden spoon, press tomatoes through strainer into a large bowl, mashing pulp and liquid through strainer. Discard tomato skins and seeds.

Place broth in a large saucepan. Bring to a boil over medium heat. Add strained tomatoes or tomato paste. In a small bowl, combine flour and sour cream. Stir 1 cup of the tomato mixture into flour mixture. Return mixture to saucepan; stir into tomato mixture until smooth. Add sugar. Season with salt to taste.

Simmer over low heat for 5 minutes. Serve hot. Garnish with parsley. ❧

Soup Crackers

Groszek Ptysiowy

Prepare these tiny crackers in advance for ease at serving time.

Makes about 72 crackers

¼ cup water
3 tablespoons butter or margarine
About 1 cup all-purpose flour
1 egg, beaten

Combine water and butter in a small skillet. Bring to a boil over medium heat. After butter melts, reduce heat to low. Slowly add 1 cup flour, stirring until mixture comes away from bottom and side of skillet, and resembles coarse meal. Remove from heat. Let cool.

Preheat oven to 425°F (220°C). Grease a baking sheet. Add egg to flour mixture. Using your hands, work egg into flour mixture and knead into smooth dough. If dough is too moist and sticky, add a little flour. Press dough into a ball. On a large lightly floured board, shape dough into 1-inch-diameter rope. Roll dough back and forth against the board, using both hands. Cut ¼-inch-thick slices from dough. Roll each slice into a small ball. Place on greased baking sheet. Bake for 15 to 20 minutes, or until golden brown. Serve in hot soups or as a garnish. ❧

Stick Crackers

Paluszki

Tasty slender crackers, these are often served with onion soup or other hot soups.

Makes about 50 crackers

¼ cup warm milk (110°F, 45°C)
1 teaspoon sugar
1 (¼-ounce) package active dry yeast (1 tablespoon)
2½ cups all-purpose flour
1 cup butter or margarine, melted, cooled
½ teaspoon salt
1 egg, beaten
Poppy, sesame, or dill seeds

Combine milk and sugar in a small bowl. Stir in yeast; let stand until foamy, 5 to 10 minutes. Place flour in a large bowl. Stir in yeast mixture. Add butter and salt. Work into a soft dough. Turn out dough on a lightly floured surface. Clean and grease bowl. Knead dough until smooth and elastic, 6 to 8 minutes, adding a little flour if dough is too soft. Place dough in greased bowl. Cover with a slightly damp towel. Let rise in a warm place, free from drafts, until doubled in bulk, about 1 hour.

Grease 2 large baking sheets. Punch down dough; knead for 1 minute. Divide dough into 4 equal parts. Cover 3 parts with a damp towel. Roll remaining part into a 1-inch-diameter rope. Cut crosswise into 1-inch pieces. Roll out pieces into strips 5 to 6 inches long. Arrange on greased baking sheets, stretching strips to 7 inches. Make sure strips are of a uniform thickness. Brush with egg; sprinkle with poppy seeds. Repeat with remaining dough. Let strips rise, uncovered, for 20 minutes.

Preheat oven to 325°F (165°C). Bake crackers for 20 to 30 minutes, or until golden brown. Cool on racks. ❧

When I was growing up in Poland, you couldn't just walk into a grocery store any time of the year and pick up two or three heads of lettuce. And you can't store lettuce, even with refrigeration, for more than a week or two. So, the only time Poles could use lettuce was when it was in season, picked from their own gardens.

When lettuce is available, it's prepared in refreshing dishes, such as Fisherman's Salad. This is a combination of chopped iceberg lettuce, fresh onions or chives, chopped hard-cooked eggs, and black olives seasoned with lemon juice, dried Italian seasoning, salt, and freshly ground black pepper.

SALADS

Because there's not much of a lettuce season, other vegetables, raw and cooked, have taken up the slack. There's Tomato Salad, a dish eaten at least once a week in most homes, when tomatoes are in season. It's simply fresh tomato wedges with chopped or thinly sliced onions in vinegar, seasoned with salt and lots of black pepper, and garnished with chopped fresh parsley.

Other vegetables have salads named in their honor, including leek, radish, and cucumber. Celery root and parsley root make an appearance here, too, as do sauerkraut and apples.

There's a lot of chopping, slicing, and shredding of carrots, cucumbers, radishes, and leeks. Cold beets are found in several creations, including, of course, Beet Salad. Cabbage is used raw and cooked, and includes the red, green, and Savoy varieties.

For spreading on canapés, choose recipes such as Cheese and Leek Salad or Beet and Horseradish Relish, a powerful combination of shredded cooked beets with horseradish.

Cold Vegetable Salad is a must at Polish weddings and holiday celebrations. It's prepared from cooked parsley root, potatoes, and carrots, combined with fresh apple, dill pickle, and hard-cooked eggs. They're all blended together in a sauce of mustard and mayonnaise. Egg Salad and Chicken Salad round out party buffet tables.

Although once difficult to find, commercial salad dressings are now available in Poland, but salads are still more often livened up with freshly squeezed lemon juice, vinegar, vegetable oil or olive oil, and, at times, with sour cream. Chopped fresh or dried parsley and dill greens are always there for garnish. ❧

Beet Salad with Apple

Salatka Bunaczana z Jablkami

Beets are a Polish favorite as a side dish or salad: They're compact, attractive, and very tasty.

Makes 4 to 6 servings

4 medium beets

3 tablespoons butter or margarine

1 medium onion, finely chopped

3 apples, peeled

2 tablespoons lemon juice

1 teaspoon sugar

¼ teaspoon salt

⅛ teaspoon ground black pepper

⅛ teaspoon ground nutmeg

Cut off beet stem ends. Scrub beets; rinse clean with cold running water. Place whole beets in a saucepan. Add enough cold salted water to cover. Bring to a boil over high heat. Cook, covered, until fork-tender, about 1 hour. Drain beets. Cool beets and peel. Grate beets into a medium bowl.

Melt butter in a large skillet over medium-low heat. Add onion; sauté until tender, 5 minutes. Grate apples into a medium bowl. Mix lemon juice into apples. Add beets and apples to onion. Sauté over medium-low heat, gently stirring, until apples are tender, about 2 minutes. Season beet mixture with sugar, salt, pepper, and nutmeg.

Serve warm as a side dish with baked pork or other entrée, or chilled as a salad. ❧

Summer Salad

Salatka Wiosenna

In Poland this salad is prepared only when lettuce is in season.

Makes 6 servings

1 head iceberg lettuce, cut in thin strips

2 medium tomatoes, each cut in 8 wedges

2 small kohlrabi, peeled, cut in julienne strips

⅓ cup sour cream

1 tablespoon lemon juice

1 hard-cooked egg, cut in thin strips

2 to 3 green onions, chopped

Salt

Freshly ground black pepper

Combine lettuce, tomatoes, kohlrabi, sour cream, lemon juice, egg, and onions in a large bowl. Season with salt and pepper to taste. ❧

Red Cabbage Salad

Salatka z Czerwonej Kapusty

Apple adds its distinctive flavor to this colorful salad.

Makes 10 to 12 servings

1 medium head red cabbage, shredded (about 8 cups)

1 medium onion, cut in strips

2 medium tart apples, peeled, grated

Juice of 1 lemon

2 tablespoons olive oil

½ teaspoon sugar

Salt

Freshly ground black pepper

Parsley sprigs

2 hard-cooked eggs, cut in wedges

In a large saucepan, boil enough salted water to cover cabbage. Drop cabbage into boiling water. Cook for 5 minutes over medium-high heat. Drain; let cool. Place cabbage in a large salad bowl. Add onion, apples, lemon juice, and oil; toss to combine. Season with sugar and add salt and pepper to taste. Gently toss to combine. Arrange parsley around inner edge of bowl. Place egg wedges around salad. Cover and refrigerate until ready to serve. ✢

Cabbage Salad

Salatka z Kapusty

This salad is often prepared during winter in Poland, when other vegetables aren't available.

Makes 8 to 10 servings

1 small head Savoy cabbage, shredded

2 tart apples, peeled, shredded

2 tablespoons lemon juice

1 teaspoon salt

½ teaspoon sugar

¼ cup olive oil

⅛ teaspoon freshly ground black pepper

1 medium dill pickle, thinly sliced

2 tablespoons chopped fresh dill or parsley

Place cabbage and apples in a large bowl. Sprinkle with lemon juice, salt, sugar, oil, and pepper; toss lightly. Top with pickle slices and dill. Cover and refrigerate for 30 minutes. Serve chilled. ✢

Sauerkraut Salad

Salatka z Kiszonej Kapusty

This salad is often served with pork entrées, especially during the winter.

Makes 6 to 8 servings

   1 pound sauerkraut, drained
   2 medium carrots, shredded
   2 medium onions, chopped
   2 tablespoons olive oil
   1 teaspoon sugar
   ¼ teaspoon salt
   ⅛ teaspoon freshly ground black pepper

Place all ingredients in a medium bowl; mix lightly. Cover and refrigerate for 30 minutes. Serve chilled.❖

Sauerkraut and Red Onion Salad

Surowka z Kiszonej Kapusty i Czerwonej Cebuli

Do not rinse sauerkraut if a sour flavor is desired.

Makes 8 servings

   1½ pounds sauerkraut, rinsed once if desired
   2 tablespoons sugar
   1 large red onion, chopped
   ¼ cup olive oil
   1 teaspoon lemon juice
   1 medium red onion, thinly sliced
   2 tablespoons chopped fresh parsley

Combine sauerkraut, sugar, chopped onion, and oil. Top with lemon juice, onion slices, and parsley. Cover and refrigerate for 30 minutes. Serve chilled.❖

Radish Salad

Salatka z Rzodkiewek

Chopped dill makes an already zesty salad even better.

Makes 6 to 8 servings

1 pound radishes, thinly sliced

2 green onions, sliced

½ cup sour cream

1 tablespoon chopped fresh dill

½ teaspoon salt

Ground white pepper

Lettuce leaves

Dill sprigs

In a medium bowl, combine radishes, green onions, sour cream, chopped dill, and salt. Season with white pepper to taste. Serve chilled on lettuce leaves, garnished with dill sprigs.

Beet Salad

Salatka z Burakow

This simple recipe is prepared year-round throughout Eastern Europe and Russia.

Makes 4 to 6 servings

2 tablespoons vegetable oil

1 medium onion, chopped

1 pound shredded cooked beets

2 tablespoons white vinegar or lemon juice

Sugar

Salt

Freshly ground black pepper

Heat oil in a medium skillet over medium heat. Add onion; sauté until tender. Add beets and vinegar. Season with sugar, salt, and pepper to taste. Gently stir over low heat until heated through, 15 minutes. Remove from heat. Let stand in skillet for 15 minutes. Serve warm.

Beet and Horseradish Relish

Cwikla

This tangy blend of flavors is especially savored during the Easter and Christmas holidays.

Makes about 2 cups

 1½ pounds grated fresh cooked or canned beets
 ½ pound prepared horseradish
 2 tablespoons lemon juice
 Pinch sugar
 Pinch freshly ground black pepper
 Salt

Combine beets, horseradish, lemon juice, sugar, and pepper in a small bowl. Add salt to taste. Cover and refrigerate overnight. Serve chilled over cold meats, sausage, or sandwiches.

Celery Root Salad

Salatka z Selera

If you can't locate the celery root, you can substitute parsley root or parsnips.

Makes 6 to 8 servings

 5 to 6 young celery roots, peeled, cut in narrow strips
 1 medium onion, minced
 ½ cup olive oil
 ⅓ cup white vinegar
 2 tablespoons chopped fresh dill
 Salt

Combine celery roots and onion in a medium bowl. In a small bowl, combine oil, vinegar, and dill. Season with salt to taste. Pour oil mixture over celery root mixture. Toss evenly to coat. Cover and refrigerate for 1 hour. Serve chilled.

Variations
Add 3 tart apples, peeled and cut in narrow strips.

Instead of cutting celery roots and apples in strips, shred them.

Cottage Cheese Salad

Salatka z Twarogu

Small portions of this salad are often eaten for breakfast.

Makes 4 to 6 servings

12 ounces small-curd cottage cheese (1½ cups)
12 radishes, thinly sliced
2 tablespoons chopped fresh chives
½ teaspoon salt
⅛ teaspoon freshly ground black pepper

Combine all ingredients in a small bowl. Cover and refrigerate for 1 hour. Serve chilled. ❧

Cheese and Leek Salad

Salatka z Sera i Porow

Serve this pleasant salad for breakfast over fresh bread or as a side dish at dinner.

Makes 6 to 8 servings

1 cup Mayonnaise, page 64, or other mayonnaise
1 pound American cheese, shredded
1 leek, diced
2 tablespoons lemon juice
Salt

Combine mayonnaise, cheese, leek, and lemon juice in a medium bowl. Season with salt to taste. Cover and refrigerate for 30 minutes. Serve chilled. ❧

Leek Salad

Salatka z Porow

For variety, substitute flavored yogurt for plain yogurt. ❧

Makes 4 servings

2 large leeks, coarsely chopped
2 tart apples, peeled, grated
Juice of 1 lemon
½ cup plain yogurt
3 tablespoons milk
¼ teaspoon salt
2 tablespoons chopped walnuts
Yogurt and leek rings (optional)

Place chopped leeks and apples in a medium bowl. Sprinkle with lemon juice. In a small bowl, combine yogurt, milk, and salt. Gently stir into leek mixture. Top with walnuts. Garnish with yogurt and leek rings (if using). Cover and refrigerate until ready to serve. ❧

Tomatoes and Cucumbers in Sour Cream

Pomidory i Ogorki w Smietanie

Makes 4 to 6 servings

Polish farmers say that cucumbers should be sliced from the flower end to prevent a bitter flavor.

- 4 medium tomatoes, each cut in 8 wedges
- 1 medium cucumber, peeled, sliced
- 1 medium onion, chopped
- ½ cup sour cream
- ½ teaspoon salt
- ⅛ teaspoon ground white pepper

Combine tomatoes, cucumber, and onion in a medium bowl. In a small bowl, combine sour cream, salt, and white pepper. Stir sour cream mixture into tomato mixture until vegetables are evenly coated. Cover and refrigerate until ready to serve. ❖

Cucumber Salad

Mizeria

The Polish name for this salad shouldn't deceive you; it's not that hard to make!

Makes 4 to 6 servings

- 3 medium cucumbers, peeled, thinly sliced
- 1½ teaspoons salt
- ½ pint sour cream (1 cup)
- ⅛ teaspoon ground white pepper
- 1 tablespoon lemon juice
- 1 tablespoon chopped fresh dill

Place cucumber slices in a medium bowl. Add salt; mix lightly until salt adheres evenly to cucumber slices. Cover and refrigerate for 1 hour. Drain juice from cucumber slices. In a small bowl, combine sour cream, white pepper, lemon juice, and dill. Add to cucumber slices; gently mix. Cover and refrigerate until ready to serve. ❖

Tomato Salad

Salatka Pomidorowa

A popular salad enjoyed at many Polish dinner tables when tomatoes are in season.

Makes 4 to 6 servings

4 medium tomatoes, each cut in 8 wedges

1 large onion, chopped

¼ cup white vinegar

1 tablespoon vegetable oil

Salt

Freshly ground black pepper

1 teaspoon chopped fresh parsley (optional)

In a medium bowl, combine tomatoes, onion, vinegar, and oil. Add salt and pepper to taste. Add parsley (if using). Cover and refrigerate until ready to serve.❖

Summer Egg Salad

Wiosenna Salatka z Jaj

Yogurt gives this fresh-tasting salad just the right texture.

Makes 4 to 6 servings

½ cup plain yogurt

3 tablespoons olive oil

1 tablespoon Dijon mustard

4 hard-cooked eggs, diced

2 small onions, diced

1 cup iceberg lettuce strips

2 tablespoons lemon juice

½ teaspoon salt

½ teaspoon sugar

2 tablespoons chopped fresh parsley

2 tablespoons chopped fresh chives

Combine yogurt, oil, and mustard in a small bowl. Place eggs, onions, and lettuce strips in a medium bowl; mix lightly. Sprinkle lemon juice, salt, and sugar over egg mixture. Add yogurt mixture, parsley, and chives. Mix lightly until combined. Cover and refrigerate for 30 minutes. Serve chilled.❖

Fisherman's Salad

Salatka Rybaka

A zesty creation, it goes nicely with any fish or seafood dish.

Makes 6 servings

1 head iceberg lettuce, chopped

1 cup chopped green onion tops or chives

2 hard-cooked eggs, chopped

8 large pitted black olives, chopped

Juice from 1 lemon

1 tablespoon olive oil

1 teaspoon dried Italian seasoning

Salt

Freshly ground black pepper

Combine lettuce, onion tops, eggs, olives, lemon juice, oil, and Italian seasoning in a large bowl. Season with salt and pepper to taste. Cover and refrigerate until ready to serve.

Chicken Salad

Salatka z Kury

Serve this nutritious, versatile salad as a side dish on lettuce leaves or as a sandwich spread.

Makes 6 to 8 servings

3 cups diced cooked chicken

1 cup drained canned or thawed frozen green peas

½ cup diced radishes

¾ cup Mayonnaise, page 64, or other mayonnaise

2 tablespoons lemon juice

½ teaspoon salt

¼ teaspoon freshly ground black pepper

¼ teaspoon ground sweet paprika

Place chicken, peas, and radishes in a medium bowl. In a small bowl, stir together mayonnaise, lemon juice, salt, pepper, and paprika. Stir mayonnaise mixture into chicken mixture until evenly distributed. Cover and refrigerate for 30 minutes. Serve chilled.

Vegetable Salad

Salatka Warzywna

A party dish, savor it during winter holidays and at Easter.

Makes 8 to 10 servings

1 parsley root, halved

3 medium potatoes

3 medium carrots, halved

1 large apple

4 small dill pickles

1 celery stalk

3 hard-cooked eggs

⅔ cup cooked green peas

5 tablespoons Mayonnaise, page 64, or other mayonnaise

¼ teaspoon prepared mustard

1 teaspoon salt

Pinch ground white pepper

Place parsley root, potatoes, and carrots in a large saucepan; add water to cover. Cover and cook over medium heat until vegetables are tender, 30 minutes. Drain vegetables, discarding cooking liquid. Cool; cover and refrigerate vegetables overnight.

Peel parsley root, potatoes, carrots, apple, and pickles; cut in ¼-inch cubes along with celery and 2 of the eggs. Place cubed ingredients in a large bowl. Stir in peas.

In a small bowl, combine mayonnaise, mustard, salt, and white pepper. Gently stir into vegetable mixture. Cover and refrigerate overnight. When ready to serve, slice remaining egg. Arrange slices on salad as garnish.

Variation
Substitute 4 cups Meat Broth, page 33, for water when cooking vegetables.

Herring Salad

Salatka Sledziowa

Here's a lip-puckering version of a Polish-style herring salad full of tart flavors.

Makes 10 to 12 servings

½ pound pickled herring, skinned, boned, chopped

1 medium dill pickle, peeled, chopped

1 tart apple, peeled, shredded

½ celery root, peeled, chopped

3 tablespoons Mayonnaise, page 64, or other mayonnaise

1 tablespoon sour cream

1 tablespoon white vinegar

Salt

Freshly ground black pepper

Half-slices of white or rye bread

In a medium bowl, combine herring, pickle, apple, and celery root. In a small bowl, combine mayonnaise, sour cream, and vinegar. Gently stir into herring mixture. Season with salt and pepper to taste. Cover; refrigerate for 1 hour. Serve chilled on bread slices. ❖

Carrot and Green-Pea Salad

Salatka z Zielonego Groszku z Marchewka

It's important not to overcook the peas. Frozen peas can be boiled for 1 to 2 minutes, then chilled before use.

Makes 8 servings

2½ cups shredded carrots
1 cup cooked green peas
½ cup Mayonnaise, page 64, or other mayonnaise
1 tablespoon lemon juice
½ teaspoon sugar
½ teaspoon salt
⅛ teaspoon freshly ground black pepper
Lettuce leaves

In a medium bowl, combine carrots and peas. In a small bowl, combine mayonnaise, lemon juice, sugar, salt, and pepper. Gently stir into carrot and pea mixture. Serve chilled on a bed of lettuce. ❖

Buttered Bread Crumbs

Zarumieniona Bulka Tarta

This is the simplest recipe in the book, but it adds flavor to many dishes.

Makes enough to garnish 4 servings

2 tablespoons dry bread crumbs
1 tablespoon butter or margarine

Place bread crumbs in a small, dry skillet. Carefully cook over medium-high heat, stirring until golden. Do not burn. Remove from heat. Add butter; stir with a fork until melted. Serve warm, lightly spooning over vegetables, pierogies, or noodles. Use sparingly. ❖

Mayonnaise

Majonez

A simple thick and creamy condiment that is more flavorful than commercial mayonnaise.

Makes about 1 cup

1 egg yolk
1 teaspoon dry mustard
½ teaspoon sugar
2 tablespoons lemon juice or white vinegar
¼ teaspoon salt
1 cup vegetable oil

Place egg yolk, mustard, sugar, lemon juice, and salt in a blender or food processor fitted with a metal blade; process until smooth. While continuing to blend, add oil, a few drops at a time, until all oil is blended in. Process until smooth. Mayonnaise should be thick and creamy. Pour into a small container. Cover tightly; refrigerate for up to 2 days.

Note

Uncooked eggs should not be eaten by young children, the elderly, or anyone with a compromised immune system, because they may contain salmonella bacteria that can cause serious illness.

Pasteurized eggs are available in some markets and are safe to eat raw in sauces or desserts that are not cooked.

Throughout Polish culinary history, vegetables have had their ups and downs. The downs came centuries ago, when vegetables were considered something to be eaten only by peasants. In the sixteenth century, Polish King Sigmund I married the Queen of Italy. He brought his new wife, complete with cooks and attendants, to the Polish Court. To ease her cultural shock, the Queen imported a variety of her native Italian vegetables, mostly greens and tomatoes. At first the Queen was met with hearty laughs from Poles who remarked that "only Italians could get fat on vegetables."

But something went right, because vegetables took hold in the Polish Court and soon spread into the common Pole's diet. To this day, the Polish word for vegetables, *wloszczyzna*, means "Italian produce."

Many of the Polish cook's vegetables are grown in small backyard gardens. They are tilled by hand and watered at times with water cranked up from wells and hand-carried by children.

Beets, cabbage, cucumbers, tomatoes, and onions are popular. Also common are asparagus, Brussels sprouts, the knob-like kohlrabi, carrots, green beans, green peas, dried beans, and cauliflower.

Their table presentations are not fancy. Most vegetables are steamed or simmered in water or mixtures of sour cream, light cream, or broth. Then they are garnished with bread crumbs, sautéed in butter, chopped fresh parsley or dill, or presented in a simple sauce.

Some vegetables, such as tomatoes or cucumbers, are difficult to store and, until only recently, could be used fresh only when in season. Although home-grown onions, carrots, potatoes, and other root vegetables are still kept in earthen cellars through winter, these vegetables are now available year-round in many modern Polish groceries and markets.

Introduced into Europe from Peru, potatoes took such firm root in Poland that today more meals are served with them than without. Potatoes are mashed, baked, fried, and rendered into the famous potato pancakes topped with an agreeable combination of cottage cheese and chopped chives. The Poles love potatoes hollowed out and filled with stuffings made of cooked pork, sausage, or beef, onions, hard-cooked eggs, and sour cream.

Just as people in the West pick strawberries, blackberries, and blueberries in the wilds, people in Poland gather mushrooms. In fact, most Polish children who live on farms or in small villages learn about wild mushrooms at a young age.

Mushrooms can be gathered only twice a year, so the Poles must resort to several methods of preserving them. They pickle small and button specimens. But pickling renders them useless for most recipes

VEGETABLES AND SAUCES

requiring the natural mushroom flavor. The most popular way to store and preserve mushrooms is to dry them. They are strung together so they're not touching one another, and hung in a place where there is constant low-heat temperature and plenty of circulating air. This is usually in the kitchen near the warm radiant stove, or by a window where both sunlight and gentle cooking heat provide slow dehydration. When dried, the mushrooms are stored for use later in countless soups, stews, salads, sauces, or stuffings.

What can you say about sauces? The Polish sauce list reads like a Who's Who of Polish vegetables. There's Onion Sauce, Tomato Sauce, and many more made with sour cream, sweet cream, wine, and broth. Nothing fancy—nothing to keep the Polish cook from his or her other activities. ❧

Beets

Buraki

Select smooth, firm, beets of uniform size for this popular side dish.

Makes 6 servings

1½ pounds beets
1 tablespoon butter or margarine
1 tablespoon all-purpose flour
3 tablespoons sour cream
1 tablespoon lemon juice
Salt

Cut off beet stem ends. Scrub beets; rinse clean with cold running water. Place whole beets in a large saucepan. Add enough cold salted water to cover. Bring to a boil over high heat. Reduce heat to medium-low. Cover with a tight-fitting lid. Cook until fork-tender, 1 hour. Remove beets from cooking liquid; discard liquid. Let cool. Peel beets.

Melt butter in a medium skillet over medium-low heat. Shred beets into buttered skillet. Blend flour and sour cream in a small bowl. Gently stir sour cream mixture and lemon juice into beets. Season with salt to taste. Heat, gently stirring, until beets are hot. Serve immediately. ❖

Brussels Sprouts

Brukselka

Serve your main meat surrounded by Brussels sprouts with this tasty sauce.

Makes 4 servings

About 1 pound Brussels sprouts
1 teaspoon sugar
¼ cup milk
1 teaspoon chopped fresh dill
Dill Sauce with Sour Cream, page 70
¼ cup dry bread crumbs
2 tablespoons butter or margarine

Remove any wilted or yellow leaves from Brussels sprouts. Trim stems with a sharp knife, making a shallow cut in the bottom of each stem to promote even cooking. Rinse in cold water. Place in a medium saucepan. Add salted water to cover and the sugar, milk, and dill. Cover and simmer until almost tender, 10 to 15 minutes.

While sprouts are cooking, prepare Dill Sauce with Sour Cream. Drain sprouts. Place in a heated serving dish; keep warm.

Place bread crumbs in a small, dry skillet. Stir over medium heat until golden brown. Remove from heat. Stir in butter or margarine until combined. Spoon browned bread crumbs over Brussels sprouts. Drizzle warm dill sauce over bread crumbs. Serve hot. ❖

Dill Sauce with Sour Cream

Sos Koperkowy

Serve this basic dill sauce over roast pork, beef, or veal.

Makes about 1¾ cups

2 tablespoons butter or margarine
2 tablespoons all-purpose flour
1 cup Meat Broth, page 33, or bouillon
¾ cup sour cream
3 tablespoons chopped fresh dill
Salt

Melt butter in a small skillet over medium heat; stir in flour. Cook, stirring, until mixture bubbles. Blend in broth; bring to a boil, stirring constantly, until thickened. Stir in sour cream and dill; do not boil. Season with salt to taste. Serve warm.

Mushroom Croquettes

Krokiety Pieczarkowe

These delicious croquettes are traditionally served as a side dish with Tomato Soup, page 50.

Makes 10 to 12 croquettes

3 tablespoons butter or margarine
1 pound fresh mushrooms, finely chopped
2 medium onions, finely chopped
1 green or red bell pepper, finely chopped
2 eggs
¼ cup milk
1¼ cups seasoned dry bread crumbs
1 teaspoon salt
¼ teaspoon freshly ground black pepper
Dill Sauce with Sour Cream, page 70 (optional)
3 tablespoons vegetable oil

Melt butter in a large skillet over medium heat. Add mushrooms, onions, and bell pepper; sauté until tender. Remove from heat and let cool.

In a medium bowl, beat eggs and milk with a fork; add 1 cup of the bread crumbs. Using a fork, mix egg mixture, salt, and black pepper into onion mixture. Using your hands and a tablespoon dipped in warm water so the mushroom mixture won't stick to it, form 1½ × 3-inch-long cylindrical croquettes. If mushroom mixture is too moist to form croquettes, add a small amount of bread crumbs. In a small dish, place the remaining ¼ cup bread crumbs and gently roll each croquette in bread crumbs. Place formed croquettes on a platter until all are made; let them dry for 5 minutes.

Prepare dill sauce (if using). Heat oil in a large skillet over medium-low heat. Carefully place croquettes into hot oil and sauté croquettes, turning, until golden on all sides. Remove croquettes to a serving dish and keep hot until needed. Serve as a side dish with sauce (if using) or plain with soups. ❖

Mushroom Casserole

Zapiekanka Pieczarkowa

In Poland, this tasty dish is popular on meatless Fridays.

Makes 6 servings

¼ cup butter or margarine

1 pound fresh mushrooms, sliced

4 cups cooked noodles

4 eggs, beaten

1 teaspoon salt

¼ teaspoon freshly ground black pepper

¼ cup grated sharp Cheddar cheese (1 ounce)

2 tablespoons chopped fresh parsley

Melt 2 tablespoons of the butter in a large skillet over medium heat. Add mushrooms; sauté

until tender. Place mushrooms in a medium bowl; set aside.

Melt the remaining butter in a large skillet over medium heat. Add noodles; sauté, stirring gently, until lightly browned. Drizzle eggs over noodles. Add salt and pepper. Cook noodle mixture, stirring, until eggs are set. Reduce heat to low. Sprinkle cheese over noodle mixture. Add mushrooms. Gently stir until heated through. Garnish with parsley. Serve immediately. ❖

Mushrooms with Cream

Pieczarki w Smietanie

This delightful side dish will complement fish or poultry entrees.

Makes 4 servings

1 tablespoon butter or margarine

1 pound fresh mushrooms, sliced

1 small onion, chopped

¼ cup water

⅛ teaspoon salt

Pinch freshly ground black pepper

1 tablespoon all-purpose flour

1 cup half-and-half

Melt butter in a medium skillet over low heat. Add mushrooms, onion, and water. Cover with a tight-fitting lid. Cook until mushrooms are tender, 25 minutes, stirring occasionally. Season with salt and pepper.

In a small bowl, blend flour and half-and-half. Stir into mushroom mixture. Cook, uncovered, over medium heat, stirring frequently, until mixture thickens. Serve hot. ⚜

Carrots in Sauce
Marchewka w Sosie

During winter, families in Poland store carrots in dark root cellars.

Makes 8 to 10 servings

Béchamel Sauce, page 87
10 medium to large carrots
About 1½ cups water
½ teaspoon salt
½ teaspoon sugar
Chopped fresh parsley

Prepare Bechamel Sauce.

Cut carrots into 1½-inch-long pieces. With a sharp knife, split pieces lengthwise into wedges no wider than ⅜ inch. Place carrots, enough water to cover, salt, and sugar in a large sauce-

pan. Cover with a tight-fitting lid. Bring to a boil, cook over medium heat until tender, 25 minutes. With a slotted spoon, carefully remove carrots from liquid, reserving liquid.

Place carrots in a deep casserole or serving dish. Stir cooking liquid into Béchamel Sauce. Bring to a simmer. Immediately pour over carrots. Garnish with parsley. Serve hot. ⚜

Tender Cabbage
Kapusta Zasamazana

This old-time vegetable is as popular today as it was centuries ago.

Makes 8 servings

2 cups Meat Broth, page 33; Chicken Broth, page 35; or bouillon
1 (2-pound) head Savoy or green cabbage, shredded
1 large carrot, shredded
2 tablespoons butter or margarine
1 onion, chopped
1½ teaspoons all-purpose flour
2 tablespoons lemon juice or white vinegar
1 teaspoon salt
⅛ teaspoon freshly ground black pepper
1 teaspoon sugar

In a large saucepan, combine broth, cabbage, and carrot. Cover and simmer for 30 minutes.

Melt 1 tablespoon of the butter in a small skillet over medium heat. Add onion; sauté until tender. Stir onion into cabbage mixture.

Melt the remaining butter in a small skillet over medium heat. Add flour; stir until flour becomes golden brown. Stir ½ cup of the simmering broth into flour mixture. Add to cabbage mixture. Simmer for 15 minutes, stirring frequently. Stir lemon juice into cabbage mixture. Season with salt, pepper, and sugar. Serve hot. ❀

Asparagus

Szparagi

Select thin young spears for this quick and delicious recipe.

Makes 6 servings

2 pounds fresh asparagus

½ teaspoon sugar

¼ cup dry bread crumbs

2 tablespoons butter or margarine

1 tablespoon lemon juice

Rinse asparagus in cold water. With your fingers, snap off hard ends; discard. In a large skillet, bring ½ inch salted water to a boil. Add asparagus and sugar. Cover with a tight-fitting lid. Bring to a boil. Reduce heat to medium-low. Cook until crisp-tender, 7 minutes; do not overcook. Drain and place on a warmed serving dish; keep warm.

Place bread crumbs in a small, dry skillet. Stir over medium heat until golden brown. Stir butter or margarine into bread crumbs until combined. Stir lemon juice into crumb mixture. Spoon crumb mixture over asparagus. Serve hot.

Variation
Spoon bread crumbs over asparagus. Drizzle 1 cup Béchamel Sauce, page 87, over bread crumbs. Top with ¼ cup grated Gouda or Parmesan cheese. Broil for 3 to 4 minutes, or until cheese melts and browns. ❀

Stuffed Tomatoes

Nadziewane Pomidory

Fresh, firm home-grown tomatoes are best for this dish.

Makes 6 servings

3 tablespoons butter or margarine
½ pound fresh mushrooms, minced
2½ cups cooked ground pork, beef, or veal
2 eggs, beaten
½ cup dry bread crumbs
2 tablespoons chopped fresh dill
½ teaspoon salt
⅛ teaspoon freshly ground black pepper
⅛ teaspoon ground nutmeg
6 medium to large ripe tomatoes

Preheat oven to 350°F (175°C). Lightly grease an 8-inch-square baking dish. Melt butter in a large skillet over medium heat. Add mushrooms; sauté until tender. Add pork; sauté until meat is heated through, 5 minutes, stirring. Stir in eggs, bread crumbs, dill, salt, pepper, and nutmeg.

Slice bottoms off tomatoes; discard bottoms. With a spoon, scoop out pulp, leaving a ¾-inch shell. Stuff tomato shells with meat mixture. Arrange stuffed tomatoes in greased baking dish. Pour water around tomatoes to a depth of ¼ inch. Bake, uncovered, for 15 minutes, or until tops of meat mixture brown. Serve immediately. ❧

Stuffed Cucumbers

Ogorki Nadziewane

This unusual method of preparing cucumbers will surprise and delight your dinner guests.

Makes 4 servings

4 small to medium cucumbers, peeled
2 tablespoons butter or margarine, at room temperature
2 eggs, separated
2 tablespoons dry bread crumbs
½ teaspoon salt
1 tablespoon chopped fresh parsley
1 teaspoon all-purpose flour
½ cup sour cream
1 tablespoon chopped fresh dill

Preheat oven to 350°F (175°C). Heavily butter a medium baking dish; add 2 tablespoons water to baking dish.

Cut one-fourth off each cucumber lengthwise. Use a spoon to scoop out seeds and pulp, leaving a ¼- to ½-inch-thick shell.

In a medium bowl, combine butter and egg yolks. Stir bread crumbs, salt, and parsley into egg yolk mixture. In a medium bowl, beat egg whites until stiff peaks form. Fold beaten egg whites into egg yolk mixture. Fill cucumber shells with egg mixture.

In a small bowl, combine flour and sour cream. Stir dill into sour cream mixture. Spoon sour cream mixture over filled cucumber shells. Arrange filled cucumber shells in baking dish. Bake, covered, for 20 minutes, or until tender when pierced with a fork. Serve hot.✤

Stuffed Green Peppers

Paprika Faszerowana

Topped with steaming Tomato Sauce, these nutritious peppers make a fine entrée.

Makes 4 servings

Tomato Sauce, page 86

4 large green bell peppers

1 tablespoon butter or margarine

1 medium onion, chopped

½ pound ground beef or pork

2 tablespoons cooked long-grain white rice

1 egg, beaten

1 teaspoon salt

¼ teaspoon freshly ground black pepper

2 medium tomatoes

1 cup Beef Broth, page 34; Veal Broth, page 36; or bouillon

Prepare Tomato Sauce. Preheat oven to 350°F (175°C). Lightly grease a shallow baking dish.

Slice tops off bell peppers; dice edible parts of cut tops. With a spoon, scoop out seeds and pith; discard. Melt butter in a small skillet over medium heat. Add diced bell pepper and onion; sauté until tender. Let cool. Combine beef, rice, and onion mixture in a medium bowl. Add egg, salt, and black pepper. Stuff pepper shells with beef mixture.

Halve tomatoes vertically. Place a tomato half, cut-side down, on top of each stuffed pepper. Arrange stuffed peppers in greased baking dish. Pour broth in bottom of baking dish. Bake, covered, for 45 minutes, or until fork-tender. Serve hot with Tomato Sauce.✤

Fresh Mushroom Torte

Tort z Pieczarek

If you prefer, your own freshly made pie crust can be substituted for the frozen pie crust used in this recipe.

Makes 6 to 8 servings

1 (9-inch) frozen pie crust

1 tablespoon butter or margarine

2 medium onions, chopped

1 pound fresh mushrooms, sliced

2 eggs

½ cup sour cream

Juice of ½ lemon

½ teaspoon salt

¼ teaspoon freshly ground black pepper

Remove pie crust from freezer; let stand at room temperature until thawed, 10 minutes. Preheat oven to 400°F (205°C).

Melt butter in a large skillet over low heat. Add onions; sauté until almost tender, 3 to 4 minutes. Stir in mushrooms. Sauté onion and mushroom mixture for 10 minutes. Let cool.

In a medium bowl, briskly mix eggs, sour cream, lemon juice, salt, and pepper. Stir in mushroom mixture, gently folding to combine. Pour mixture into the pie crust. Bake for 30 minutes, or until mushroom mixture is set firm throughout. Cut into wedges. Serve hot.

Potato Pancakes

Placki Kartoflane

The pancakes may also be served topped with Hungarian Goulash, page 160.

Makes 35 to 40 pancakes

Cottage-Cheese Topping

12 ounces cottage cheese (1½ cups)

¼ cup chopped fresh chives

7 large new potatoes, peeled (about 3 pounds)

1 medium onion

1 egg, beaten

3 tablespoons all-purpose flour

¾ teaspoon salt

⅛ teaspoon freshly ground black pepper

Vegetable oil

Prepare Cottage-Cheese Topping: In a small bowl, combine cottage cheese and chives; set aside.

Preheat oven to 350°F (175°C). Using a hand grater or food processor fitted with a shredding blade, shred potatoes to make about 4½ cups. Squeeze potatoes to remove any liquid, reserving liquid in a small bowl. Place potatoes in a large bowl. Depending on age and type of potatoes used, up to 1 cup juice may be obtained.

Finely grate onion. Stir together potatoes, onion, egg, flour, salt, and pepper. Discard top portion of reserved potato juice, leaving juice about ½ inch deep or about ¼ cup. This bottom juice contains potato starch. Stir reserved juice into potato mixture.

In a large skillet, heat about 3 tablespoons oil over medium-high heat. Drop 1 heaping tablespoon of the potato mixture into skillet. Smooth out into a pancake 2½ to 3 inches round. Place as many pancakes as possible in skillet. Cook until browned and crisp on bottom, about 3 minutes. Turn and cook other side until brown and crisp. Remove from skillet and drain on paper towels.

When drained, transfer to a heatproof serving plate; keep hot in a warm oven. Add oil to skillet as necessary. Serve hot with Cottage-Cheese Topping.❧

Potato Cutlets

Kotlety Ziemniaczane

A fast, easy way to prepare potatoes to serve for any meal.

Makes 12 cutlets

Mushroom Sauce, page 86
2 pounds potatoes, boiled in skins, peeled
1 egg
¼ cup all-purpose flour
½ cup dry bread crumbs
¼ cup vegetable oil

Prepare Mushroom Sauce; keep warm.

Grind, shred, or mash potatoes into a large bowl. Blend in egg and flour. Spread bread crumbs on a work surface. Using your hands, shape potato mixture into a smooth log about 12 inches long. Roll log in bread crumbs, pressing bread crumbs evenly into outer surface. Slice potato log into 1-inch-thick pieces. Press remaining bread crumbs into cut sides of cutlets.

Heat oil in a large skillet. Add cutlets; fry until both sides are browned, 5 minutes on each side. Serve immediately, topped with warm Mushroom Sauce.❧

Potato Surprise

Niespodzianka Ziemniaczana

Select smooth, long potatoes of equal size.

Makes 10 servings

10 medium to large baking potatoes

¼ cup butter or margarine

1 medium onion, chopped

2½ cups ground cooked meat

1 egg, beaten

1 tablespoon chopped fresh parsley or 1 teaspoon dry parsley flakes

½ teaspoon salt

⅛ teaspoon freshly ground black pepper

1 tablespoon ground sweet paprika

2 cups gravy or Mushroom Sauce, page 86 (optional)

Cook potatoes in water to cover over medium-high heat for 15 minutes. Remove potatoes from water; discard water. Let potatoes cool.

Preheat oven to 400°F (205°C). Grease a shallow baking dish. Peel potatoes. Lengthwise, cut top one-fifth off each potato; reserve tops. Carefully hollow out each potato, leaving a ½-inch-thick shell; reserve potato flesh for other use.

Melt 2 tablespoons of the butter in a medium skillet over medium heat. Add onion; sauté until tender. Blend in meat, egg, parsley, salt, and pepper. Stuff potatoes with meat mixture; replace tops.

Arrange potatoes in greased baking dish. Bake, uncovered, for 15 minutes. Melt remaining 2 tablespoons butter in a small saucepan; stir in paprika. Brush mixture lightly over potatoes. Bake for 45 minutes, or until tender when pierced with a fork. Serve hot with gravy (if using). ⚜

Stuffed Potatoes

Nadziewane Ziemniaki

Makes 5 servings

5 medium to large baking potatoes

3 tablespoons butter or margarine

1 medium onion, chopped

1 cup chopped cooked lean beef, pork, or sausage

1 hard-cooked egg, chopped

1 tablespoon sour cream

Salt

Freshly ground black pepper

Scrub potatoes; pat dry with paper towels. Cut 1½ inches off one end of each potato; reserve ends. Carefully hollow out each potato with a thin-bladed knife and spoon, leaving a ½-

inch-thick potato shell. Reserve potato flesh for other use.

Preheat oven to 350°F (175°C). Melt 1 tablespoon of the butter in a small skillet over medium heat. Add onion; sauté until tender. In a small bowl, combine onion, meat, egg, and sour cream.

Stuff potato shells with meat mixture. Recap potatoes by replacing ends; secure with wooden picks. Melt the remaining 2 tablespoons butter in a small skillet. Brush each potato with butter.

Arrange potatoes on a rack in a baking dish. Bake for 1 hour, or until tender when pierced with a fork. To serve, slice lengthwise. Sprinkle with salt and pepper to taste.

Potato Bake
Zapiekanka Ziemniaczana

For interesting variations, try topping this recipe with different kinds of cheese.

Makes 8 to 10 servings

6 medium or large baking potatoes, peeled, quartered
3 medium carrots, chopped
1 medium onion, chopped
¼ cup butter or margarine
½ to ¾ cup milk
½ teaspoon salt
⅛ teaspoon ground white pepper
1½ cups grated Cheddar cheese (6 ounces)
Ground sweet paprika

Cook potatoes, carrots, and onion in salted water to cover until all vegetables are tender, 20 minutes. Drain and discard cooking water.

Preheat oven to 400°F (205°C). Grease a 13 × 9-inch baking dish. Mash vegetables, adding butter and enough milk to form a mixture with a consistency a little softer than typical mashed potatoes. Season with salt and pepper.

Arrange potato mixture in the greased dish. Sprinkle cheese on top of potato mixture. Garnish with paprika. Bake, uncovered, for 35 minutes, or until lightly browned. Serve hot.

Holiday Potatoes

Swiateczne Ziemniaki

This was an easy recipe for my mother to make; that's where the name "holiday" came from.

Makes 6 to 8 servings

  3 pounds potatoes (10 to 12 medium potatoes)
  1 (8-ounce) package cream cheese, at room temperature
  2 eggs, beaten
  ⅔ cup sour cream
  ⅓ cup light cream
  1 teaspoon ground white pepper
  6 tablespoons butter, room temperature
  ¼ cup finely chopped onion
  ¼ cup finely chopped green bell pepper
  ¼ cup finely chopped red bell pepper
  Ground paprika, to garnish

Preheat oven to 350°F (175°C). Grease a large shallow casserole with butter. Peel and cut potatoes into small equal-size pieces. Cook potatoes in boiling salted water until tender, about 20 minutes. Drain and mash while still hot. Add cream cheese and mix well. Stir eggs, sour cream, light cream, and white pepper into potato mixture.

Melt 4 tablespoons of the butter in a small skillet over medium heat. Add onion and bell peppers. Sauté until onion is tender, 2 minutes; remove from heat and let cool. Mix vegetables into potatoes. Evenly place potato mixture into buttered casserole. Distribute remaining 2 tablespoons butter on top of potatoes and garnish with a little paprika. Bake, uncovered, for 1 hour, or until top of potato mixture is crispy and partly browned. Serve hot.❧

Mom's Homefries

Babcia's Kartoffel

If desired, use a heavy cast-iron skillet or baking pan that could be started on the stove top, and then transferred to the oven or broiler to cook from the top so potatoes won't need turning.

Makes 4 to 6 servings

  6 medium potatoes
  3 tablespoons vegetable oil
  2 medium onions, finely chopped
  1 pound fresh mushrooms, thinly sliced
  ½ pound bacon, cooked and crumbled
  1 cup light cream
  1 tablespoon all-purpose flour
  1 teaspoon salt
  ½ teaspoon freshly ground black pepper
  2 tablespoons finely chopped fresh parsley

Wash, peel, and thinly slice potatoes; pat dry with paper towels. In a large skillet, heat oil over medium-high heat. Arrange potatoes in a layer in the skillet. Arrange onions evenly over potatoes. Distribute mushrooms evenly over onions. Sprinkle bacon over mushrooms. Trickle light cream over potato mixture. Mix flour, salt, pepper, and parsley in a small bowl; sprinkle over potato mixture. Cook over medium-high heat until potato bottoms are cooked and browned, about 5 minutes. Using a large turner, carefully turn potato and mushroom mixture. Cook until mushrooms and onions are tender, 5 minutes. Turn potatoes a third time. Cook until some of the potatoes turn crispy, 2 minutes. Serve hot. ❖

Babcia's Potato Cake

Babka Ziemniaczna

This dish can serve as a breakfast meal within itself, or an interesting side dish along practically any entrée.

Makes 6 to 8 servings

1 tablespoon butter or margarine

1 medium onion, minced

3 cloves garlic, minced

3 tablespoons vegetable oil

4 pounds potatoes

2 tablespoons all-purpose flour

1 teaspoon salt

½ teaspoon white pepper

2 eggs

1 pound bacon slices

Melt butter in a medium skillet over medium heat. Add onion and garlic; sauté until onion is tender. Let onion and garlic cool.

Preheat oven to 350°F (175°C). Grease a baking pan with the 3 tablespoons vegetable oil. Peel and finely grate potatoes onto a fine-mesh cheesecloth. Gather grated potatoes in the cloth and squeeze with your hands over the sink or a bowl, discarding any squeezed liquid. Place potatoes in a large mixing bowl. Stir onion and garlic, flour, salt, and pepper into potatoes. In a medium bowl, beat eggs with a fork; combine with potato mixture.

Fry bacon in a skillet over medium heat until crisp; pat dry. Spoon potato mixture into prepared pan. Place bacon strips, whole or crumbled, on top of potato mixture. Bake, uncovered, for 1½ hours, or until a wooden pick inserted in the center of potato mixture comes out clean. Serve hot. ❖

Tomato Bake

Zapiekanka Pomidorowa

The pie crust for this recipe can be used for any recipe calling for a homemade pie crust.

Makes 1 (9-inch) pie, 6 servings

Pie Crust, or l frozen (9-inch) pie shell

    1 cup all-purpose flour

    ½ teaspoon salt

    1/16 teaspoon baking powder

    ¼ cup vegetable shortening

    3 tablespoons cold milk

1½ cups grated Cheddar cheese (6 ounces)

1 cup chopped fresh spinach

3 medium to large ripe tomatoes, cut into ¼-inch-thick slices, unpeeled

½ cup diced onion

½ cup diced green bell pepper

½ cup diced red bell pepper

About ¼ cup mayonnaise

Prepare crust: Preheat oven to 400°F (205°C). Sift flour, salt, and baking powder together onto a flat, dry working surface. Using a pastry blender or 2 knives, cut shortening into a texture similar to that of coarse cornmeal. Add milk to the flour mixture a little at a time, working dough with a fork until a fairly stiff ball can be formed. Place dough ball on a floured pastry cloth or other floured flat surface. Using a floured rolling pin, roll dough, from center to edge, into a 10-inch circle about ⅛ inch thick. Carefully fold dough in half and lift into a 9-inch pie pan. Unfold dough so it fits into the pan. Trim edges if dough overhangs. Bake for 5 minutes, or until golden brown. Cool. Or bake a frozen pie crust according to package directions and cool.

Preheat oven to 350°F (175°C). Sprinkle ½ cup of the cheese evenly on bottom of crust. Sprinkle spinach on top of cheese. Neatly arrange sliced tomatoes on top of the spinach in equal layers. Sprinkle onion and green and red bell peppers over tomato layers. Sprinkle another ½ cup of the cheese over vegetables. Drizzle mayonnaise evenly over cheese and vegetables. Sprinkle remaining ½ cup cheese over top. Bake, uncovered, for 35 minutes. Remove from heat. Let stand for 10 minutes before serving. Cut into 6 pieces and serve warm.

Grits with Vegetables

Kasza z Warzynami

Makes 6 to 8 servings

3 tablespoons butter or margarine

1 cup dry grits

1 medium onion, finely chopped

1 pound fresh mushrooms, sliced

⅛ teaspoon ground cayenne pepper

1 tablespoon chopped fresh parsley

1 quart Chicken Broth, page 35, or Beef Broth, page 34

Preheat oven to 350°F (175°C). Melt 2 tablespoons butter in a large nonstick skillet. Add grits, onion, mushrooms, cayenne, and parsley. Sauté over medium heat, stirring occasionally, until vegetables are tender and grits are slightly browned, 5 minutes. Grease a large casserole with remaining 1 tablespoon butter. Transfer grits and vegetables to buttered casserole; add broth. Bake grits and vegetables for 1½ hours, or until broth is absorbed and vegetables are tender. Serve hot.

Victory Rice

Ryz Viktoria

This dish is an excellent companion to Fresh Dill Soup, page 43.

Makes 4 to 6 servings

2 cups Chicken Broth, page 35; Beef Broth, page 34; or bouillon

1 cup uncooked long-grain white rice

½ cup dry bread crumbs

1 cup fresh or frozen green peas

1 pound smoked ham

Pinch salt

Pinch freshly ground black pepper

4 eggs, beaten

1 cup grated mild Cheddar cheese (4 ounces)

Preheat oven to 300°F (150°C). Heavily butter bottom and sides of an 8-inch-square baking dish.

In a medium saucepan, bring broth to a boil. Add rice; cover with a tight-fitting lid. Cook over medium heat for 10 minutes. Evenly sprinkle bread crumbs over bottom of baking dish. Spoon cooked rice over bread crumbs; smooth top of rice. Spoon peas over rice in an even layer. Slice ham into thin strips. Place on top of rice and peas. Season with salt and pepper. Pour eggs over ham. Sprinkle cheese on top of eggs. Bake, uncovered, 50 minutes, or until lightly browned. Serve hot.

Cumberland Sauce

Sos Cumberland

A little of this flavorful sweet sauce goes a long way.

Makes about 1¼ cups

1 orange

5 tablespoons red wine

¼ cup currant jelly

¼ cup apple juice or cider

2 teaspoons prepared mustard

Grate orange peel into a medium saucepan. Squeeze juice from orange; set aside. Add wine to peel; cook over medium heat for 2 minutes. Add jelly, orange juice, apple juice, and mustard. Beat with a wire whisk until jelly is melted and mixture is frothy. Pour into a small serving bowl. Serve over roast turkey or duck.❖

Madeira Sauce

Sos Maderowy

This sauce will turn inexpensive meat cuts into expensive-tasting dishes.

Makes about 1¾ cups

3 tablespoons butter or margarine

1½ tablespoons all-purpose flour

1 cup Meat Broth, page 33, or bouillon

1 tablespoon Maggi seasoning

⅔ cup Madeira wine

½ teaspoon sugar

Salt

Freshly ground black pepper

Melt butter in a small skillet over medium heat. Stir in flour and cook until golden brown. Blend in broth and Maggi seasoning. Simmer over low heat for 15 to 20 minutes, stirring frequently. Add Madeira wine and sugar. Simmer over low heat for 5 minutes, stirring constantly. Season with salt and pepper to taste. Serve hot.❖

Horseradish Sauce

Sos Chrzanowy

This sauce will spice up meat, fish, egg, or casserole dishes.

Makes about 2¼ cups

2 tablespoons butter or margarine
1 tablespoon all-purpose flour
½ pint sour cream (1 cup)
2 tablespoons prepared horseradish
1 cup Meat Broth, page 33, or bouillon
½ teaspoon lemon juice
1½ teaspoons sugar
Salt

Melt butter in a small skillet; stir in flour. Cook over medium heat until golden brown. Let cool. Stir cooled flour mixture into sour cream. Blend in horseradish.

Heat broth in a small saucepan. Add sour cream mixture, lemon juice, and sugar. Season with salt to taste. Heat until hot; do not boil. Remove from heat. Cool slightly. Serve warm.

Onion Sauce

Sos Cebulowy

Serve over roast lamb or veal.

Makes about 1½ cups

2 tablespoons butter or margarine
5 medium onions, finely chopped
½ cup Chicken Broth, page 35; Beef Broth, page 34; or bouillon
2 tablespoons all-purpose flour
½ cup half-and-half
½ teaspoon sugar
Salt

Melt butter in a medium skillet over medium heat. Add onions; sauté until tender. Using a spoon, press cooked onions and juices through a strainer into a medium bowl. Stir in broth.

In a small bowl, blend flour and half-and-half; stir into strained onion mixture. Add sugar. Return to skillet. Cook over low heat, stirring constantly, until mixture bubbles and thickens. Season with salt to taste. Serve warm.

Tomato Sauce

Sos Pomidorowy

Serve over hot sliced roast veal or pork.

Makes 3 to 3¼ cups

Béchamel Sauce, page 87
1 cup Meat Broth, page 33, or bouillon
2 tablespoons tomato paste
1 teaspoon sugar
½ teaspoon ground sweet paprika

Prepare Béchamel Sauce. Combine broth, Béchamel Sauce, and tomato paste in a medium saucepan. Stir in sugar and paprika. Cook over medium heat for 5 minutes, stirring constantly.

Variation

For a milder flavor, stir 2 beaten egg yolks into warm sauce and cook over low heat, stirring, until slightly thickened.❖

Mushroom Sauce

Sos Pieczarkowy

Excellent served over rice, noodles, potatoes, or meat.

Makes about 4½ cups

2 tablespoons butter or margarine
1 pound fresh mushrooms, thinly sliced
1 medium onion, chopped
2 tablespoons all-purpose flour
2 cups Chicken Broth, page 35; Beef Broth, page 34; or bouillon
¼ teaspoon salt
¼ teaspoon freshly ground black pepper
½ pint sour cream (1 cup)

Melt butter in a large saucepan. Add mushrooms and onion. Cover with a tight-fitting lid; simmer over low heat for 15 minutes, stirring occasionally. Stir flour into mushroom mixture until blended. Stir in broth. Cover and simmer over low heat for 30 minutes. Season with salt and pepper. Stir sour cream until blended; add to mushroom mixture, a little at a time, stirring until smooth. Cook over medium-low heat for 2 minutes; do not boil. Serve hot.❖

Béchamel Sauce

Sos Beszamelowy

This recipe can be used to make a wide variety of other sauces.

Makes about 2 cups

2 tablespoons butter or margarine

2½ tablespoons all-purpose flour

1¾ cups milk

½ teaspoon salt

Pinch ground white pepper

Pinch ground nutmeg

1 tablespoon Maggi seasoning

Juice of 1 lemon

Melt butter in a medium saucepan over low heat. Stir in flour until smooth. Cook, stirring, until bubbles begin to form. Gradually add milk, stirring constantly. Bring to a simmer. Stir in salt, white pepper, nutmeg, and Maggi seasoning. Cook over medium heat until thickened, 5 to 7 minutes. Stir lemon juice into sauce. Serve hot over meat, potatoes, or vegetables.

Mayonnaise Sauce

Sos Majonez

This sauce is excellent over hot baked potatoes.

Makes about 2 cups

½ cup shredded provolone cheese (2 ounces)

4 ounces cottage cheese (½ cup)

1 cup Mayonnaise, page 64, or other mayonnaise

1 tablespoon lemon juice

Chopped fresh parsley (optional)

In a blender or food processor fitted with a metal blade, blend provolone and cottage cheese. Add mayonnaise and lemon juice; process until blended. Place in a small serving dish. Serve at room temperature. Garnish with parsley (if using).

Of all Polish foods, none are more versatile than pierogies. From Polish, *pierogi* translates to "small pies" in English. But in any language, pierogies are a culinary delight, to be served as a main or side dish, snack, or even as a dessert.

Pierogies have always been popular in Poland because they can be made with a seemingly endless variety of fillings, depending on what is available at the moment. With food supplies what they were in Poland, this came in handy to the village housewives who years ago had to use all their resources to make the best of a poor situation.

If you've had pierogies before, you know how delicious they are. If you have yet to savor a pork, cheese, or cabbage pierogi, you're in for a tasty surprise.

Contrary to popular belief, good pierogies are not difficult to make. Simple ingredients make up the dough, and the fillings are easily prepared using little more than a hand grinder.

When you begin making pierogies, a hand grinder is preferred over a blender or food processor because it is easier to control. Once you get a feel for the consistency that results from a hand grinder, you can switch to a more modern grinding method, if desired.

Helpful Hints for Making Pierogies

For most pierogies, make the dough after the savory filling has been prepared. However, when using a

PIEROGIES AND DUMPLINGS

fruit filling, prepare dough first. That way the juice won't be drawn out of the fruit prematurely while waiting for the dough to be completed. When boiling fruit pierogies, simmer them in water for an additional 10 to 15 minutes.

All pierogies can be frozen for future use. You can dust unboiled pierogies with flour and freeze them in airtight containers. Or place unboiled pierogies on baking sheets and freeze them for 20 to 30 minutes. Then store them in plastic bags or other containers in a freezer. If you want to save time later, another alternative is to boil and drain pierogies, let them cool, and then freeze.

Most savory pierogies, especially pork, mushroom, and cabbage, will benefit when sautéed with thinly sliced onions in butter.

When serving, brush fruit pierogies with melted butter or softened cream cheese.

A close relative of the pierogi is the *uszka*, or "little ear." For all practical purposes, uszkas may be considered a Polish version of ravioli. These small filled dumplings are most commonly prepared with ground leftover cooked pork, beef, or veal, mixed with bread crumbs and sautéed onions. Mushroom filling is popular for meatless holidays like Christmas Eve and certain days during Lent. Regardless of the filling, uszkas provide tasty additions to hot clear soups, or can be eaten by themselves, sautéed in butter like pierogies.

Another recipe that calls for fillings is *nalesniki*. Translated to "crepes," these thin rounds of cooked batter are made from eggs and flour. They can be rolled jelly-roll style or folded like pockets or envelopes around fillings of dry cottage cheese and chopped chives, or a zesty combination of chicken, mushrooms, and onions.

Kulebiak means "fingers," but is prepared in a long roll that is sliced into individual serving pieces. Its filling consists of dried mushrooms, sauerkraut, onions, and chopped hard-cooked eggs. Kulebiak can be served hot or cold.

Unfilled noodles include String Noodles, the batter of which is trickled into boiling broth or soup, and Round Dumplings, which are plain dumplings garnished with sautéed bread crumbs or crumbled crisp bacon. ❖

String Noodles

Lane Kluski

These are simple-to-make, no-fuss noodles.

Makes enough noodles for 6 to 8 servings

2 eggs
¼ cup all-purpose flour
Boiling broth or soup

Beat eggs in a medium bowl. Stir in flour.

Drizzle batter into boiling broth while stirring gently. Batter will cook into noodles within the hot liquid in less than 1 minute. ❧

Lazy Noodles

Leniwe Kluski

Polish cooks use farmer's cheese—a type of cottage cheese that's pressed into a soft but solid loaf (unlike American farmer's cheese, which is a hard block or brick of cheese). When Polish farmer's cheese cannot be found, regular cottage cheese will work—as long as it's well drained. Cooked noodles can be added to soups or served as a side.

Makes about 6 cups

2 eggs
1 pound regular cottage cheese, well drained, or Polish-style farmer's cheese
1 teaspoon salt
3½ to 4 cups all-purpose flour
Grated Parmesan cheese, to serve (optional)
Grated mozzarella cheese, to serve (optional)
Salt
Freshly ground black pepper

In a food processor, process eggs until blended. Add cottage cheese and salt and process until smoothly blended. To cottage cheese mixture, add flour, ½ cup at a time, processing each time, until 2½ cups of flour have been added and processed into a smooth, sticky dough. Remove dough from food processor and place on a flat, lightly floured surface. Work dough with hands, adding additional ½ cup of flour until dough is smooth enough to be worked into rope pieces about ½ inch thick. Using 45-degree angle cuts, cut dough ropes into pieces about 1½ inches long.

In a large pot, bring about 8 quarts water to a boil over medium-high heat. Add about one-third of dough pieces, gently stirring them with a slotted spoon so they won't stick to each other or the bottom of the pot. Boil, uncovered, until all pieces float, about 6 minutes per batch. Lightly oil a large serving dish or container; using a slotted spoon, transfer cooked noodles to dish. Return cooking water to a boil; add another one-third of dough pieces to boiling water. Repeat cooking process. Serve noodles as a side dish, sprinkling with Parmesan and mozzarella cheeses (if using), or season with salt and pepper to taste.✥

Filled Potato Dumplings
Nadziewane Kluski Ziemniaczane

These dumplings make a wonderful meal by themselves, and can be served at any meal; they make excellent leftovers as well.

Makes 14 to 16 filled dumplings

Dumpling Filling
   1 pound lean ground beef round or ½ pound lean ground beef and ½ pound lean ground pork
   2 tablespoons butter or margarine
   1 medium onion, minced
   1 clove garlic, minced
   1 teaspoon salt
   ¼ teaspoon freshly ground black pepper
   1 egg, lightly beaten
   ½ cup dry bread crumbs
Dough
   2 medium potatoes, baked and cooled
   10 to 12 medium potatoes, peeled
   1 teaspoon salt
   ½ to 1 cup all-purpose flour

   2 tablespoons butter or margarine
   1 medium onion, chopped
   1 pound sliced bacon, placed in freezer for
   30 minutes before use

Prepare filling: Place meat in a large bowl; set aside. Melt butter in a medium skillet over medium heat. Add onion, garlic, salt, and pepper; sauté until onion is tender, about 2 minutes. Remove from heat and let cool. Add onion mixture, egg, and bread crumbs to meat. Combine with your hands into a smooth filling.

Prepare dough: Peel baked potatoes. Mash and press peeled baked potatoes through a sieve into a large bowl. Grate raw potatoes into another bowl. Strain grated potatoes through a fine-mesh cheesecloth, allowing potato juices, with potato starch, to collect in a medium bowl. Let potato juices and starch stand for 10 minutes so starch collects in the bottom of the bowl. Meanwhile, mix strained potatoes, mashed potatoes, and salt in another bowl. Carefully tip bowl with potato juice so liquid runs off, leaving starchy liquid in the bowl. Add remaining starch liquid to potato mixture. Mix flour with potato a little at a time until a smooth, pliable dough forms.

To form dumplings, wet your hands with cool water. Take ¼ cup dough and roll in a ball between your hands. Flatten the dough into a circular shape, then place 1 tablespoon filling in the center of the dough round, and evenly shape dough around the filling into a round dumpling about 3 inches in diameter by about 2 inches thick. Set completed dumpling aside. Repeat process, occasionally wetting your hands so dough will not stick to your skin.

Bring water to a boil in a large pot. Add dumplings, one at a time, to boiling water. Gently stir so they won't stick to the pot or each other. Simmer until dumplings float, then cook for 15 minutes, stirring occasionally. Remove dumplings with a slotted spoon and arrange on a warmed serving dish. Melt butter in a medium skillet over medium heat. Add onion and sauté until tender; set aside. Remove partly frozen bacon from freezer; cut slices into ½-inch square pieces. Sauté bacon in a large skillet over medium heat until almost crisp. Drain well. Spoon onion and bacon over dumplings. Serve warm.

Variation

Slice dumplings in two halves or four quarters and sauté in 2 tablespoons vegetable oil until filling and dough are browned on one or more sides. Serve hot with sautéed onions and cooked bacon. This works especially well for leftover dumplings a day or two later. ❧

Potato Dumplings

Pyzy

These dumplings can also be served with crumbled crisp-cooked bacon and sautéed onions.

Makes 70 to 75 dumplings

4 pounds potatoes, peeled
1 teaspoon salt
1 egg

In a medium saucepan, place one-third of the potatoes with enough salted water to cover. Bring to a boil over high heat. Reduce heat to medium. Partially cover; cook until tender, 20 minutes. Drain; let cool. Grind cooked potatoes into a large bowl; set aside. Grate remaining raw potatoes onto a piece of doubled cheesecloth about 20 × 12 inches. Gather ends of cheesecloth so grated potatoes are enveloped in a ball. Squeeze excess potato juice into a medium bowl by twisting cheesecloth ends. Reserve potato juice. Stir squeezed raw potatoes into cooked potatoes. Add 1 teaspoon salt and egg. Work mixture together 3 to 4 minutes. From reserved potato juices, spoon off all but bottom 2 tablespoons potato juice, which contains potato starch. Stir bottom 2 tablespoons juice into potatoes.

Bring a pot of salted water to a boil over medium heat. Using your hands, roll 1 heaping teaspoon of the potato mixture into a ball. Drop potato dumplings into boiling water. Boil until potatoes are cooked and dumplings float, about 7 minutes.

Variation
Stuffed Potato Dumplings: Press 1 tablespoon potato mixture in your hand into a flat round. Place ½ teaspoon Meat Filling for Pierogies, page 102, in center. Roll potato mixture in a ball around filling. Cook as above. Makes 25 to 30 dumplings. ❧

Round Dumplings

Kluski Kladzione

These are excellent as leftovers the next morning, sautéed in butter.

Makes 4 to 6 servings

1 egg
2 tablespoons water
¾ cup all-purpose flour
⅛ teaspoon salt
2 to 3 tablespoons buttered bread crumbs or crumbled crisp-cooked bacon

Beat egg in a medium bowl. Add water; beat until smooth. Gradually add flour, beating constantly until smooth. Beat in salt.

In a large stockpot, bring 5 to 6 inches of salted water to a boil over medium-high heat. Dip a teaspoon in boiling water to prevent dough mixture from sticking to it. With the wet teaspoon, drop 1 scant teaspoon dough into boiling water. Dip spoon in water again; repeat process until all dough is used. Cover pot with a tight-fitting lid. Bring to a boil. Cook over medium-high heat until all dumplings float, 10 minutes. Watch carefully, as liquid will easily boil over.

Pour dumplings into a colander. Rinse with hot water. Garnish with bread crumbs or bacon. Serve hot with soups or as a side dish to meat.

Variation
Substitute ½ teaspoon onion salt for ⅛ teaspoon salt. Or add 2 teaspoons minced onion or chives. ❧

Cheese-Filled Crepes

Nalesniki z Serem

These light, nourishing creations are often served for breakfast.

Makes 16 to 18 crepes

Cheese Filling
    1 pound dry cottage cheese or ricotta cheese
    (2 cups)
    ½ cup chopped fresh chives
    1 egg, beaten
    1 egg yolk
    Salt
    White pepper
Crepes
    3 eggs
    1 cup water
    1 cup milk
    1½ cups all-purpose flour
    ½ teaspoon salt
    Butter or margarine

Prepare Cheese Filling: In a grinder or food processor, grind cheese. Do not overprocess or puree. In a medium bowl, stir together cheese, chives, egg, and egg yolk. Season with salt and white pepper to taste.

Make the crepes: In a large bowl, beat eggs for about 1 minute. Add water, milk, flour, and salt. Beat into a smooth batter.

Grease a crepe pan or 7-inch skillet with butter. Heat greased pan or skillet over medium heat. Pour a scant ¼ cup of batter onto center of hot pan. Tip pan so batter is evenly distributed. Cook over medium heat until lightly golden. Turn and cook briefly until golden. Do not brown. Remove from pan and place on a platter. Repeat process until all batter is used, greasing pan as necessary.

Fill and fold the crepes using one of the following methods: 1. Spread 1 tablespoon of filling on half of a crepe; roll crepe starting on filling side. 2. Spread 1 tablespoon of filling over half of crepe; fold crepe in half, then in half again. 3. Spread 1 tablespoon of filling over center of crepe, leaving a 1-inch border; fold one-third of crepe over filling, then fold in other one-third of crepe and fold ends in, forming a packet.

Melt 1 tablespoon butter in a large skillet. Place as many filled crepes as will fit in skillet without crowding. Cook over medium heat until both sides are golden, 3 to 4 minutes on each side. Place on a warm platter. Cook remaining crepes, adding butter as needed. Serve hot.

Variation
Sweet Cheese Filling: Substitute 5 tablespoons sugar, 1 teaspoon melted butter or margarine, and 1 tablespoon vanilla extract for chives, salt, and pepper in above filling recipe. ⚜

Chicken and Mushroom Crepes
Nalesniki z Kury z Grzybami

If you prefer, substitute chopped cooked pork or beef for chicken.

Makes 10 to 12 crepes or 5 to 6 servings

Chicken and Mushroom Filling
  3 tablespoons butter or margarine
  ½ pound fresh mushrooms, chopped
  1 medium onion, chopped
  3 tablespoons water
  2 cups diced cooked chicken
  Salt
  White pepper

  Béchamel Sauce, page 87 (optional)

Crepes
  2 cups all-purpose flour
  ½ teaspoon salt
  ½ teaspoon ground white pepper
  ¼ teaspoon ground nutmeg
  2 egg yolks
  1 cup milk
  ¾ cup water
  2 teaspoons Maggi seasoning
  3 egg whites
  Butter or margarine

  2 eggs
  1 cup dry bread crumbs
  1 to 2 tablespoons butter or margarine
  Chopped fresh parsley (optional)

Prepare Chicken and Mushroom Filling: Melt butter in a large skillet over medium heat. Add mushrooms, onion, and water; sauté until mushrooms and onion are tender. Stir chicken into mushroom mixture. Reduce heat to medium-low. Cook, stirring, until mixture is heated through and lightly browned, 10 minutes. Season with salt and white pepper to taste. Remove from heat; let cool.

Prepare Béchamel Sauce (if using).

Make the crepes: In a large bowl, combine flour, salt, white pepper, and nutmeg. In a small bowl, combine egg yolks, milk, water, and Maggi seasoning. Stir egg yolk mixture into dry ingredients, making a smooth batter. Beat for at least 5 minutes. In a medium bowl, beat egg whites until stiff peaks form. Fold beaten egg whites into batter until evenly distributed.

Grease a crepe pan or 7-inch skillet with butter. Heat greased pan or skillet over medium heat. Pour ⅓ cup of batter into hot pan or skillet. Using a round bottom of a spoon, smooth out batter to a 7- or 8-inch circle. Cook over medium to medium-low heat for about 2 minutes. Turn with a spatula. Cook for 1 to 2 minutes on other side. Do not brown or overcook as they will lose their pliability. Remove from pan; place on a platter. Repeat with remaining batter, adding butter as needed.

Fill and fold crepes following one of the methods used for Cheese-Filled Crepes, page 95.

Beat eggs in a shallow medium bowl until blended. Place bread crumbs in a pie plate. Dip filled crepes in beaten egg, then in bread crumbs, pressing crumbs evenly onto surface of crepes. Melt butter in a large skillet over medium heat. Place as many filled crepes, seam side down, as will fit in skillet without crowding. Cook until both sides are golden, 3 to 4 minutes on each side. Place on a warm platter. Cook remaining crepes, adding butter as needed. Serve hot, with Béchamel Sauce (if using). Garnish with parsley (if using).

Variation
Preheat oven to 375°F (190°C). Grease a large shallow baking dish. After sautéing crepes, arrange in greased baking dish. In a small bowl, combine 1 cup sour cream, 2 tablespoons shredded sharp Cheddar cheese, and ¼ teaspoon curry powder. Spread over crepes. Bake, uncovered, for 10 to 12 minutes, or until sour cream mixture has a dull sheen. Serve immediately.

Kulebiak

Kulebiak

This is a baked, rolled dough filled with a delicious mushroom-sauerkraut mixture.

Makes 2 rolls

Kulebiak Filling

 1 ounce dried mushrooms

 2 pounds sauerkraut, drained

 2 tablespoons butter or margarine

 2 large onions, minced

 3 hard-cooked eggs, chopped

 Salt

 Freshly ground black pepper

 2 (¼-ounce) packages active dry yeast
 (2 tablespoons)

 ¼ cup warm water (110°F, 45°C)

 1½ teaspoons sugar

 About 4 cups all-purpose flour

 ¾ cup warm milk (110°F, 45°C)

 1 tablespoon butter or margarine, melted

 ⅛ teaspoon salt

 ⅛ teaspoon ground nutmeg

 2 eggs, slightly beaten

 1 egg white, beaten

Prepare Kulebiak Filling: Place mushrooms in a medium saucepan; add water to cover. Let stand for 6 to 8 hours or overnight. Cook mushrooms in soaking water, covered, over medium-low heat until tender, 1 hour. Strain liquid into a small bowl; reserve liquid. Finely chop

mushrooms. Place sauerkraut and mushroom liquid in a large saucepan. Cook, uncovered, over medium heat until liquid evaporates, 10 minutes, stirring occasionally.

Melt butter in a large skillet over medium heat. Add onions; sauté until tender. Stir in mushrooms, sauerkraut, and eggs. Season with salt and pepper to taste. Cook over medium heat for 5 minutes. Let cool.

In a small bowl, dissolve yeast in warm water. Stir in sugar and 1 tablespoon of the flour. Let stand until foamy, 5 to 10 minutes. Beat in milk, butter, salt, nutmeg, eggs, and 2 cups of the flour. Stir in enough remaining flour to make a soft dough, Turn out dough onto a lightly floured surface. Clean and grease bowl. Knead dough until smooth and elastic, 8 to 10 minutes. Place dough in greased bowl, turning to coat all sides. Cover with a damp cloth. Let rise in a warm place, free from drafts, until doubled in bulk.

Preheat oven to 350°F (175°C). Grease a large baking sheet. Punch down dough. Divide dough in half. On a lightly floured surface, roll out half the dough to a 14 × 12½-inch rectangle. Spread half of the filling over rolled dough, leaving a 1-inch border. Roll dough lengthwise, jelly-roll style. Crimp ends closed by pinching them together. Tuck ends under. Carefully place filled Kulebiak on greased baking sheet. Repeat with remaining dough and filling.

Pierce each Kulebiak with a fork to allow steam to escape. Brush Kulebiak with egg white. Bake for 45 minutes, or until golden brown. Let cool slightly. Cut in ¾- to 1-inch slices. ✣

Pierogies

Pierogi

For variety, make each batch of these "small pies" with two different fillings.

Makes about 70

Pierogi fillings, pages 100 to 103

4 cups all-purpose flour

2 eggs

5 tablespoons sour cream

6 tablespoons vegetable oil

Pinch salt

About ¾ cup water

Sautéed onions for savory pierogies, and melted butter or softened cream cheese for fruit pierogies

Prepare choice of pierogi fillings.

Lightly flour 2 baking sheets. Sift flour into a large bowl or onto a flat work surface; make a well in the center. Break eggs into well. Add sour cream, 3 tablespoons of the oil, and salt.

Blend ingredients with your fingertips. Gradually add water, working and kneading mixture into a smooth, pliable dough.

Divide dough into quarters. Cover three portions with a damp cloth. On a lightly floured board, roll out dough portion into a ¹⁄₁₆-inch-thick rectangle. Cut into 3½- to 4-inch circles.

In center of 1 dough circle, place 1 heaping tablespoon filling. Fold dough in half over filling. Crimp resulting edge with your fingertips, forming a tight seal. Repeat process until remaining dough is used, placing pierogies on lightly floured baking sheet.

Bring a large saucepan of salted water to a boil, using ½ teaspoon salt per 2 quarts water. Drop about 5 pierogies into boiling water. Stir gently to prevent them from sticking to the bottom. When water returns to a boil, add 5 more pierogies. Stir carefully. Cover with a tight-fitting lid. Cook savory pierogies over medium heat until they float, 4 to 5 minutes. Cook fruit pierogies for 10 to 15 minutes. Gently remove pierogies from pot; drain in a colander or strainer. Rinse with hot water. Repeat until all pierogies are boiled. Pat pierogies dry with paper towels.

For savory pierogies, heat remaining 3 tablespoons oil in a large skillet. Add 10 boiled pierogies; sauté over medium heat until browned on both sides, 5 to 6 minutes. Place in a large ovenproof serving dish. Keep hot in oven. Sauté remaining pierogies. Serve hot, garnished with sautéed onions (if using). Serve boiled fruit pierogies brushed with melted butter or softened cream cheese. ❧

Blueberry Filling for Pierogies

Nadzienie z Czarnych Jagod

Use fresh blueberries for this delicious filling.

Makes about 4 cups or enough to fill 40 to 45 pierogies

4 cups fresh blueberries
1 tablespoon sugar

Wash berries; drain. In a medium bowl, sprinkle berries with sugar. Mix lightly. Fill pierogi shells immediately, before juice is drawn out of fruit.

Variation
Substitute 4 cups fresh blackberries, raspberries, or sliced strawberries for blueberries. ❧

Cherry Filling for Pierogies

Czeresniowe Nadzienie

Use fresh sweet or tart cherries for this popular summer pierogi filling.

Makes about 4 cups or enough to fill 40 to 45 pierogies

4½ cups dark sweet or red tart cherries
1 teaspoon lemon juice for sweet cherries
Sugar to taste for tart cherries

Wash, drain, and pit cherries. Lightly press cherries in a strainer or colander to remove some juice. Place cherries in a medium bowl. If sweet cherries are used, sprinkle with lemon juice. If tart cherries are used, add sugar. Fill pierogi shells immediately, before juice is drawn out of fruit. ❧

Vanilla-Cheese Filling for Pierogies

Pierogi Waniliowe

With this filling, pierogies can be used as either a main dish or dessert.

Makes about 4 cups or enough to fill 40 to 45 pierogies

> 2 pounds dry cottage cheese or ricotta cheese
> (4 cups)
> 1 egg yolk
> ¼ cup seedless raisins
> 1 teaspoon vanilla extract
> Pinch salt
> 2 tablespoons sugar or to taste

Using a grinder or food processor fitted with a metal blade, process cheese. Do not puree or process too fine. In a large bowl, combine cheese, egg yolk, raisins, vanilla, salt, and sugar.

Cheese Filling for Pierogies

Pierogi z Serem

Polish farmers make their own cottage cheese from curdled milk.

Makes about 4 cups or enough to fill 40 to 45 pierogies

> 2 pounds dry cottage cheese or ricotta cheese
> (4 cups)
> 1 egg plus 2 egg yolks, beaten
> ½ teaspoon salt
> Pinch ground white pepper

Using a grinder or food processor fitted with a metal blade, process cheese. Do not puree or process too fine. In a large bowl, combine cheese, egg and egg yolks, salt, and white pepper. Stir to combine.

Variation
Sweet Cheese Filling: Add ¼ cup sugar and omit pepper. Stir until smooth. Serve hot filled pierogies with whipped cream.

Meat Filling for Pierogies

Pierogi z Miesem

Pork is the most popular of all meat fillings in Poland.

Makes about 4 cups or enough to fill 40 to 45 pierogies

1 pound ground cooked pork, lamb, veal, or beef
(about 4 cups)
2 tablespoons butter or margarine
1 medium onion, chopped
2 eggs, beaten
½ teaspoon salt
½ teaspoon freshly ground black pepper

Using a grinder or food processor fitted with a metal blade, process meat. Do not puree or process too fine. Melt butter in a large skillet over medium heat. Add onion; sauté until tender. Stir in meat and eggs. Sauté for about 5 minutes. Season with salt and pepper. Let cool.❧

Sauerkraut Filling for Pierogies

Pierogi z Kapusty Kwaszonej

Sauerkraut pierogies are traditionally served as a Christmas Eve main dish.

Makes about 4 cups or enough to fill 40 to 45 pierogies

1 pound sauerkraut
2 tablespoons butter or margarine
1 medium onion, chopped
Pinch salt
Pinch freshly ground black pepper

In a medium saucepan, place sauerkraut and enough water to cover. Simmer, uncovered, over low heat for 30 minutes. Drain well. Using a grinder or food processor fitted with a metal blade, process sauerkraut. Do not puree or process too fine. Melt butter in a large skillet over medium heat. Add onion; sauté until tender. Blend in sauerkraut, salt, and pepper. Let cool.❧

Fresh Mushroom Filling for Pierogies

Pierogi z Pieczarkami

Use this filling for other dishes besides pierogies.

Makes about 4 cups or enough to fill 40 to 45 pierogies

¼ cup butter or margarine

2 pounds fresh mushrooms, minced

2 medium onions, minced

¼ cup dry bread crumbs

½ teaspoon salt

½ teaspoon freshly ground black pepper

Melt 2 tablespoons of the butter in a large skillet. Add mushrooms; sauté over low heat until tender, stirring occasionally. Place mushrooms in a medium bowl. Melt remaining 2 tablespoons butter in skillet. Add onions; sauté over medium heat until tender. Let cool. Stir in bread crumbs. Stir mixture into mushrooms. Season mixture with salt and pepper.✤

Polish Ravioli

Uszka

Fill these miniature dumplings with almost anything you want.

Makes about 115 ravioli

Ravioli fillings, page 104

2½ cups all-purpose flour

⅛ teaspoon salt

1 tablespoon butter or margarine, chilled

1 cup boiling water

1 egg yolk, lightly beaten

Prepare choice of ravioli fillings.

In a medium bowl, combine flour and salt. Using a pastry blender or 2 knives, cut butter into flour until mixture resembles coarse crumbs. Pour boiling water over mixture. Blend with an electric mixer until smooth, at least 5 minutes. Let cool. Blend in egg yolk. Cover and refrigerate 1 hour or longer.

Divide dough into 8 equal portions. On a lightly floured board, roll 1 piece of dough into a ¹⁄₁₆-inch-thick rectangle. Cut into 2-inch squares. Place about 1 teaspoon filling in center of each square. Fold each square in half diagonally to form a triangle. Pinch edges together; crimp closed. Fold 2 corners of longest edge so they overlap. Press overlapping corners together and crimp.

Bring a large saucepan of salted water to a boil, using ½ teaspoon salt per 2 quarts water. Drop about 10 ravioli into boiling water. Stir gently to prevent them sticking to the bottom. When water returns to a boil, add 10 more ravioli. Depending on size of pot, after 40 to 60 ravioli have been added, cover with a tight-fitting lid; cook over medium-high heat for 4 to 5 minutes. Remove with a slotted spoon. Serve like Pierogies, page 99, or serve in hot soup. ❖

Meat Filling for Ravioli

Uszka z Miesem

Meat can be leftovers from pork, beef, or veal roasts, or meat used in broth-making.

Makes enough filling for about 115 ravioli

3 tablespoons butter or margarine

1 large onion, minced

½ pound ground cooked meat (about 2 cups)

¼ cup Meat Broth, page 33, or bouillon

¼ cup dry bread crumbs

1 egg, lightly beaten

Melt butter in a medium skillet over medium heat. Add onion; sauté until tender, 3 to 5 min-

utes. Add meat, broth, and bread crumbs. Cook, uncovered, over medium heat for about 10 minutes, stirring constantly. Let cool. Blend in egg. ❖

Mushroom Filling for Ravioli

Uszka z Grzybami

For a delightfully different flavor, rehydrate dried mushrooms in red wine.

Makes enough filling for about 115 ravioli

3 ounces dried mushrooms

2 tablespoons butter or margarine

3 medium onions, minced

¾ teaspoon salt

¼ teaspoon freshly ground black pepper

2 tablespoons dry bread crumbs

1 egg white, lightly beaten

Place mushrooms in a medium bowl; add water to cover. Let stand for 6 to 8 hours or overnight. Grind mushrooms in a hand grinder. Melt butter in a medium skillet over medium heat. Add onions; sauté until tender 3 to 5 minutes. Add mushrooms, salt, pepper, and bread crumbs. Cook, uncovered, over medium heat for about 15 minutes, stirring constantly. Let cool. Blend in egg white. ❖

Poultry

If you visit Poland, you might be surprised at how often chicken is served in homes and restaurants. When most people think of Polish main dishes, they think of pierogies, stuffed cabbage, kielbasa, or pork recipes. Although those dishes certainly are important, the true culinary workhorse of the Polish kitchen is the common chicken.

Polish housewives appreciate the fact that chicken is one of the most versatile meats available. Its nutritious, sweet, delicious meat can be breaded and fried, sautéed, roasted, stewed, and used to make croquettes, patties, and casseroles. Chicken can be enjoyed hot or cold, and its leftovers are welcome in any home.

During the two decades I lived in Poland, I can't remember my mother ever buying chickens at a grocery store. Like thousands of others who owned small farms or houses with tiny fenced-in yards, we raised our own.

Once each spring, my mother would hitch our horse and wagon and travel seven miles to town to pick up a wide, flat boxful of 70 to 80 chirping "peeps," baby chicks that would eventually provide nourishing, delicious meat and eggs for our family throughout the year.

Families in Poland that don't raise their own birds depend on their poultry "know-how" when they purchase chicken for the table. Even in cities like Warsaw and Cracow, most chickens are bought live or freshly killed from neighboring village farmers, or in the countryside at one of the many farmer's markets that open for business at the crack of dawn.

Because chicken is relatively easy to obtain in Poland—compared with red meats—a large variety of chicken dishes exist. As mentioned earlier, Chicken Soup ranks number one on the popularity list. Chicken breasts are breaded and fried, or ground after cooking and made into patties or slender, bite-size Chicken Fingers, which are also breaded and fried. A favorite Sunday dish is roast chicken cooked with a delicious stuffing containing mushrooms cooked in wine.

POULTRY AND EGGS

Turkeys are not considered a staple in Poland. These big birds are sometimes stuffed, but usually are roasted for the holidays. They're rubbed with a mixture of oregano, paprika, cloves, salt, and pepper and stuffed with pieces of apple, celery, carrot, and green pepper.

Eggs

Although most Polish cooks rate the chicken before the egg on their popularity list, eggs nonetheless are close behind. They're indispensable for baking and play major and minor roles in appetizers, soups, salads, vegetables, and many other dishes. Indeed, you'll find eggs within every chapter of this book. Naturally, they also provide the ingredients from which light, nourishing main dishes are prepared.

Although the eggs Poles use in cooking are neither uniform in size, color, or even shape, one trait is characteristic of all. The eggs are deliciously fresh, gathered by children who go through the barn chasing hens off their nests, some of which are built high in lofts. On many occasions, in order to come up with the freshest egg, my youngest brother would hide near a nesting hen and patiently wait for the moment of truth.

The egg dish most often prepared in Poland is scrambled eggs cooked with chunks of smoked pork loin. It's to be eaten at breakfast with fresh rolls or bread spread with hard white butter.

But there are also omelets made with pieces of kielbasa, ham, mushrooms, peas, spinach, and even herring. Like elsewhere, in Poland eggs are fried, soft-boiled, poached, and baked in little ramekins with cream and minced ham.

Eggs play an important role in traditional Easter celebrations in the Polish household. Eggs are colored fancily with the same beeswax-and-dye system made popular by the Ukrainians, or plainly, using onion skin, beet juice, and wild-root dyes. Every Easter godparents bring children baskets filled with candy, presents, and colored eggs. The children make a contest of cracking colored egg against colored egg until only one—the winning egg—is left unscathed. ❖

Chicken in Vegetable Sauce

Kura w Sosie Warzywnym

Every Polish household cook has a similar version of baked chicken and vegetables that's an absolute staple in the family.

Makes 4 to 6 servings

About 3 pounds chicken legs or other pieces
1 cup all-purpose flour
1 tablespoon commercial seasoning blend such as Mrs. Dash, or a combination of 2 tablespoons chopped fresh parsley, 1 teaspoon salt, ½ teaspoon black pepper, and ¼ teaspoon cayenne pepper or paprika
¼ cup vegetable oil
1 large onion, chopped
2 large carrots, chopped
1 medium zucchini squash or yellow squash, chopped
½ pound chopped fresh mushrooms
1 quart Chicken Broth (page 35)
About 6 cups cooked rice or noodles (optional)

Preheat oven to 325°F (165°C). Wash chicken pieces and pat dry. Mix flour and seasoning in a medium bowl. Roll chicken pieces in flour mixture; place on a baking sheet. In a large nonstick skillet, heat oil over medium-high heat. Add chicken pieces. Sauté, turning pieces, until evenly browned, about 1 minute on each side. Remove chicken from heat and arrange in a large baking pan.

To the skillet, add onion, carrots, squash, and mushrooms. Sauté over medium heat until onion is tender, 5 minutes. Stir remaining flour mixture into cooking vegetables and cook until bubbly. Stir chicken broth into vegetables. Simmer, stirring, over low heat until thickened and bubbly.

Place chicken in baking pan; pour vegetable sauce over chicken. Bake for 1 hour, or until chicken is tender. To serve, arrange chicken pieces on a large platter, over a bed of cooked rice or noodles (if using). Spoon hot vegetable sauce over chicken.

Chicken in Spicy Cream Sauce

Kura w Ostrym Sosie Smietanowym

This tasty combination of chicken and cream is spiced with garlic, paprika, and lemon.

Makes 4 servings

2 large cloves garlic, crushed

1 tablespoon salt

½ teaspoon ground sweet paprika

1 (3- to 3½-pound) chicken, quartered

3 tablespoons vegetable oil

1 cup half-and-half

2 tablespoons lemon juice

1 tablespoon chopped fresh parsley

Combine garlic, salt, and paprika in a small bowl. Rub chicken pieces with garlic mixture. Let stand for 15 minutes. Heat oil in a large skillet over medium heat. Add chicken; cook chicken until both sides are browned, 10 minutes on each side. Combine half-and-half and lemon juice in a small bowl; spoon over chicken. Cover and simmer until tender, 1 hour, turning once. Place chicken in a warm serving dish. Spoon hot cooking juices over chicken. Garnish with parsley. ❧

Chicken Fingers

Paluszki z Kury

These handsome tidbits will outdo any chicken finger food you'll find in restaurants, wings down.

Makes 20 pieces or 4 servings

4 chicken breast halves, skinned, boned

2 tablespoons ground sweet paprika

1 tablespoon salt

1 teaspoon freshly ground black pepper

About 1 cup dry bread crumbs

2 eggs

Vegetable oil

Cut each chicken piece lengthwise in 5 equal strips. Place each chicken strip between plastic wrap. Using a meat mallet, pound chicken strips until about ¼ inch thick.

In a heavy plastic bag, combine paprika, salt, and pepper. Add chicken strips; shake to coat evenly. Or spread strips on a flat surface; sprinkle evenly with paprika mixture. Arrange seasoned strips on a baking sheet. Let stand for 15 minutes.

Place bread crumbs in a shallow dish. In a small, shallow bowl, beat eggs. Dip seasoned chicken strips in eggs, then in bread crumbs. Pour oil ½ inch deep in a large skillet. Heat to 350°F (175°C), or until a 1-inch bread cube turns golden brown in 65 seconds. Fry coated chicken strips in hot oil until golden brown, 2 to 3 minutes, turning once. Drain on paper towels. Serve hot. ✧

Vienna Chicken

Kurczak po Wiedensku

Poles love the tasty flavor of fresh garlic offered in this simple dish, and so will you!

Makes 6 servings

1 (4- to 4½-pound) chicken, skinned, boned
5 cloves garlic, minced
1 tablespoon salt
¼ teaspoon freshly ground black pepper
2 eggs
1 tablespoon half-and-half, whipping cream, or milk
½ cup all-purpose flour
About 1 cup dry bread crumbs
Vegetable oil
Butter or margarine, at room temperature
Fresh parsley sprigs

Cut chicken in serving-size pieces. Place chicken pieces between plastic wrap. Using a meat mallet, pound about 3 to 4 times on each side.

Combine garlic, salt, and pepper in a small bowl. Rub chicken all over with garlic mixture. Let stand for 15 minutes.

Place eggs and half-and-half in a small, shallow bowl. Lightly beat with a fork. Place flour and bread crumbs in separate shallow dishes. Roll a chicken piece in flour, then dip in beaten egg and roll in bread crumbs. Press crumbs evenly onto chicken. Place coated chicken on a wire rack. Repeat with remaining pieces. Let stand for 15 to 20 minutes at room temperature to firm coating. Or refrigerate until ready to cook.

Preheat broiler. Pour oil ¼ inch deep in a large skillet. Heat oil over medium heat. Add chicken; fry until both sides become golden brown, 5 to 6 minutes, turning once. Drain on paper towels. Arrange fried chicken in a large, shallow baking dish. Place a small dab of butter on each piece. Broil chicken for 2 minutes. Garnish with parsley. Serve immediately. ✧

Chicken Roll with Vegetables

Kurcze z Jarzynami

If you can't find parsley root, substitute a parsnip in the vegetable filling.

Makes 5 to 6 servings

10 chicken breast halves, skinned, boned

2 tablespoons butter or margarine

3 medium carrots, finely chopped

2 medium onions, finely chopped

1 parsley root, finely chopped

1¼ cups Chicken Broth, page 35, or bouillon

2 eggs, beaten

¼ cup frozen or fresh cooked green peas

Salt

Freshly ground black pepper

Place chicken breast halves between plastic wrap. Using a meat mallet, pound until chicken is about ¼ inch thick. Trim each chicken piece into a rectangular shape, cutting away about one-fourth of the meat. Finely chop trimmed meat.

Melt butter in a large skillet. Add carrots, onions, parsley root, and ¼ cup of the broth. Sauté over medium heat until cooking juices are reduced to about 2 tablespoons, 15 minutes. Reduce heat to low. Stir eggs and peas into vegetables. Simmer until eggs set, stirring constantly. Add chopped chicken. Season with salt and pepper to taste. Sauté for 3 to 4 minutes. Remove from heat; let cool.

Preheat oven to 325°F (165°C). Grease a 13 × 9-inch baking dish. Evenly spread cooked chicken mixture on flattened chicken breast rectangles. Roll chicken pieces from short end, jelly-roll style. Secure with wooden picks. Place chicken in greased dish seam sides down. Pour the remaining 1 cup broth over chicken. Cover and bake for 40 to 50 minutes, or until fork-tender. ❖

Chicken in Flames

Kura w Plomieniach

Prepare this dramatic dish for an intimate candlelight dinner.

Makes 4 servings

1 (3- to 3½-pound) chicken

1 tablespoon salt

Stuffing

4 stale dinner rolls

½ cup milk

¼ cup butter or margarine

2 eggs

1 teaspoon salt

¼ cup dry bread crumbs

1 tablespoon finely chopped walnuts

1 tablespoon finely chopped almonds

1 teaspoon ground nutmeg

¼ cup chopped fresh parsley

2 tablespoons strong Polish vodka or other vodka

Rub chicken, inside and out, with salt; let stand for 15 minutes.

Prepare Stuffing: In a medium bowl, soak rolls in milk. In a food processor fitted with a metal blade, process soaked rolls, butter, eggs, salt, bread crumbs, walnuts, almonds, nutmeg, and parsley until combined.

Preheat oven to 375°F (190°C). Grease a deep baking dish. Fill chicken body cavity with stuffing. Place stuffed chicken in greased dish. Cover and bake for 30 minutes. Remove cover; bake for 30 minutes. or until juices run clear when a knife is inserted between breast and thigh.

Using a heavy cleaver or knife, cut chicken in quarters. Place chicken quarters, skin side up, on a platter. Pour vodka over chicken. Using a long match, carefully ignite vodka. Serve immediately.

Baked Chicken with Mushrooms

Kura Pieczona z Pieczarkami

The combination of sweet onions and tangy sour cream creates a special dinner treat.

Makes 4 to 6 servings

1 (3- to 3½-pound) chicken, cut up
1 teaspoon salt
¼ cup all-purpose flour
4 tablespoons butter or margarine
1 teaspoon ground sweet paprika
2 medium onions, chopped
2 cups Chicken Broth, page 35, or bouillon
½ pound fresh mushrooms, sliced
1 cup sour cream
2 tablespoons chopped fresh parsley

Rub chicken pieces with salt; let stand for 15 minutes.

Preheat oven to 325°F (165°C). Grease a 13 × 9-inch baking dish. Place flour in a shallow dish. Roll chicken pieces in flour until evenly coated. Melt 3 tablespoons of the butter in a large skillet over medium heat. Add chicken; sauté until chicken browns on all sides. Arrange chicken in greased baking dish; reserve pan juices. Sprinkle paprika evenly over chicken.

Add onions to skillet. Sauté over medium heat until tender. Spoon onions over chicken. Pour broth over chicken. Cover and bake for 45 minutes. Melt the remaining 1 tablespoon butter in a medium skillet over medium heat. Add mushrooms; sauté until tender. Spoon mushrooms over chicken. Spoon sour cream over chicken. Sprinkle with parsley. Cover; bake for 15 to 20 minutes, or until chicken is tender. ❧

Chicken with Mushroom Stuffing

Kura z Pieczarkowym Nadzieniem

Mushrooms cooked in white wine bring a wonderful flavor to this inexpensive dish.

Makes 4 servings

Mushroom Stuffing

 2 cups white wine

 3 tablespoons butter or margarine

 1 pound fresh mushrooms, sliced

 1 chicken liver, minced

 1 cup stale bread cubes or croutons

 ¼ teaspoon freshly ground black pepper

 ¼ teaspoon ground nutmeg

 ½ teaspoon salt

 2 tablespoons chopped fresh parsley

 2 eggs, beaten

 1 (3- to 3½-pound) chicken

 Salt

 Ground sweet paprika

 Freshly ground black pepper

Gravy

 1 tablespoon Maggi seasoning

 ½ cup white wine

 1 cup Chicken Broth, page 35, or bouillon

 1 tablespoon cornstarch

 2 tablespoons water

Prepare Mushroom Stuffing: Heat wine and 1 tablespoon of the butter in a large skillet over medium-low heat. Add mushrooms; cook until tender. Remove mushrooms from cooking juices; set aside. Add liver to cooking juices. Cook over medium-low heat until tender. Remove liver; set aside. Reserve cooking juices for gravy.

Melt the remaining 2 tablespoons butter in a large skillet over medium heat. Add bread; sauté until bread begins to brown. Let cool. Stir mushrooms, liver, pepper, nutmeg, salt, and parsley into bread. Add eggs. Lightly mix with a fork to combine; set aside.

Preheat oven to 350°F (175°C). Lightly rub chicken, inside and out, with salt. Fill chicken cavity with stuffing. Lightly sprinkle paprika and pepper over outside of chicken. Place chicken in a roasting pan. Cover and roast for 1 hour. Uncover; roast for 30 minutes, or until juices run clear when a knife is inserted between breast and thigh. Place chicken on a platter.

Prepare Gravy: In a small saucepan, combine reserved cooking juices, Maggi seasoning, wine, and broth. Blend cornstarch and water in a small bowl. Stir into broth mixture. Simmer over low heat, stirring constantly, until thickened, 10 minutes. Serve gravy on the side.

Chicken Patties with Poached Eggs

Kotlety z Kury z Jajkami

When turning these patties in the skillet, be careful so they don't break apart.

Makes 6 servings

¼ cup milk

1 stale dinner roll

1 pound cooked chicken, minced

1 egg

½ teaspoon salt

¼ teaspoon freshly ground black pepper

½ teaspoon ground nutmeg

1 tablespoon chopped fresh parsley

3 tablespoons butter or margarine, melted

½ cup dry bread crumbs

Vegetable oil

6 eggs

Place milk in a large bowl. Break roll into pieces; soak roll pieces in milk. Mash soaked roll. Blend in chicken, egg, salt, pepper, nutmeg, parsley, and butter.

Shape chicken mixture into 6 (4- to 5-inch-round) patties. Place bread crumbs in a shallow dish. Carefully press both sides of each patty into crumbs until evenly coated. Heat 3 tablespoons oil in a large skillet over medium heat. Add 3 patties; fry until both sides are browned, 3 to 4 minutes on each side. Place browned patties on a plate: keep warm in oven. Brown remaining chicken patties, adding oil as needed.

Poach eggs in a large saucepan of simmering water to desired doneness, 4 to 6 minutes. To serve, carefully place 1 poached egg on each chicken patty.

Chicken Paprika

Paprykarz z Kury

A simple, fast, and zesty dish, it is usually served with rice.

Makes 6 servings

6 to 8 chicken breast halves, skinned, boned

2 tablespoons butter or margarine

2 medium onions, sliced

1 teaspoon ground sweet paprika

Pinch salt

Pinch freshly ground black pepper

1½ cups Chicken Broth, page 35, or bouillon

3 tablespoons sour cream mixed with 2 teaspoons all-purpose flour

Place chicken pieces between plastic wrap. Using a meat mallet, pound each piece to about ⅜ inch thick. Melt butter in a large skillet over medium heat. Add half of the chicken to skillet; sauté for 3 minutes per side. Remove chicken and set aside. Cook remaining chicken. Remove and add to other chicken, reserving pan juices in skillet.

Add onions, paprika, salt, and pepper to skillet with pan juices. Sauté over medium heat until onions are tender, 10 minutes. Return chicken to skillet. Add broth. Cover and simmer for 15 minutes. Transfer chicken to a platter and keep warm. Stir in sour cream mixture. Simmer, uncovered, until liquid just begins to bubble, 5 minutes; do not boil.❖

Baked Cornish Hens
Mlode Kurczaki

For best results, select firm, ripe tomatoes.

Makes 4 servings

¼ cup butter or margarine

4 Cornish hens, thawed, if frozen, cut in halves

5 cloves garlic, crushed

1 tablespoon salt

¼ teaspoon freshly ground black pepper

⅛ teaspoon ground thyme

1½ cups dry white wine

4 medium tomatoes, peeled, sliced, and seeded

1 tablespoon potato starch or cornstarch mixed with 1 tablespoon water

Preheat oven to 350°F (175°C). Melt butter in a large skillet over medium-low heat. Add hen pieces; sauté until both sides are golden brown, 10 minutes on each side. Arrange hen pieces in a shallow baking dish. Add cooking juices; sprinkle with garlic, salt, pepper, and thyme.

Cover and bake for 20 to 25 minutes. Add wine to cooking juices. Arrange tomatoes over hen pieces. Cover; bake for 15 minutes, or until tender. Transfer hen pieces to a warm platter.

Pour ¼ cup of the cooking juices into a small saucepan. Stir in potato starch or cornstarch mixture until well blended. Pour in remaining cooking juices. Bring to a boil over medium heat, stirring constantly, until thickened. Reduce heat to low. Simmer for 5 minutes. To serve, spoon sauce over hen pieces.❖

Cornish Hens Kaukas

Kurczaki po Kaukasku

This spicy recipe originated in a mountainous region of Russia.

Makes 4 servings

6 cloves garlic, minced
About 2 teaspoons ground sweet paprika
2 tablespoons salt
½ teaspoon freshly ground black pepper
4 Cornish hens, thawed, if frozen
3 tablespoons vegetable oil
1 cup half-and-half
2 tablespoons lemon juice

In a small bowl, combine garlic, paprika, salt, and pepper. Rub hens, inside and out, with garlic mixture.

Heat oil in a large deep skillet over medium heat. Brown hens evenly. In a small bowl, combine half-and-half and lemon juice; pour over hens. Place skillet over low heat. Cover with a tight-fitting lid. Simmer until hens are tender, about 1 hour, turning hens once every 15 minutes. Serve hot.

Goose with Prunes

Ges ze Sliwkami

This is a simple but effective method to cook your goose!

Makes 8 to 10 servings

1 tablespoon salt
1 teaspoon freshly ground black pepper
1 teaspoon ground marjoram
1 (8- to 9-pound) goose, thawed, if frozen, cut up
¼ cup butter or margarine, melted
¾ pound dried, pitted prunes, soaked overnight in water to cover

Combine salt, pepper, and marjoram in a small bowl. Rub goose pieces all over with salt mixture. Let stand for 20 minutes.

Add goose and butter to a large skillet over medium heat. Sauté until browned on both sides. Add prunes. Cover with a tight-fitting lid. Reduce heat to medium-low. Simmer until tender, 1 to 1½ hours, turning goose pieces every 15 minutes. To serve, place goose on a warm platter. Spoon cooked prunes and juices over goose.

Goose Ragout

Pikantne Ragout z Gesi

Try to find a grain-fed goose about five or six months old for this main dish.

Makes 8 to 10 servings

3 cups Chicken Broth, page 35, or bouillon
1 (8- to 9-pound) goose, thawed, if frozen, then cut up
2 medium carrots, chopped
1 leek, chopped
1 parsley root, chopped
1 celery root, chopped
1½ teaspoons salt
½ teaspoon freshly ground black pepper
¼ teaspoon ground thyme
½ ounce dried mushrooms, chopped
2 tablespoons butter or margarine
2 medium onions, chopped
2 tablespoons tomato paste
1 tablespoon all-purpose flour
½ cup red wine
Cooked white rice

Heat broth in a large saucepan. Add goose. Cover with a tight-fitting lid. Simmer over low heat for 45 minutes, turning several times. Add carrots, leek, parsley root, celery root, salt, pepper, thyme, and mushrooms. Cook, covered, over low heat until goose is tender, 1 hour. Remove goose from pan; let cool for 10 minutes. Reserve cooking liquid and vegetables.

Remove goose meat from bones; discard bones. Cut cooked goose meat into bite-size pieces. Melt butter in a large skillet over medium-low heat. Add onions; sauté until tender. Stir tomato paste, flour, and wine into onions. Add goose meat, reserved vegetables, and cooking liquid. Bring to a boil over medium heat. Serve over hot rice.

Roast Duckling

Nadziewana Kaczka

The sweet-and-sour Cumberland Sauce adds just the right touch to the distinctive roast-duckling flavor.

Makes 2 to 4 servings

1 (4½- to 5-pound) duck, thawed, if frozen
1 teaspoon salt
3 cloves garlic, minced
½ cup water
3 medium apples, cored
Cumberland Sauce, page 84

Preheat oven to 350°F (175°C). Remove giblets and neck from duck cavity. Rinse duck under cold running water; pat dry with paper towels. Remove any excess fat from duck; discard fat. Prick duck skin all over to let fat drain during roasting. Rub duck, inside and out, with salt and garlic. Place duck, breast side up, on a rack in a shallow roasting pan. Pour water in bottom of roasting pan. Place whole apples in duck cavity.

Roast duck for 1½ to 2 hours, or until juices run clear when a knife is inserted between breast and thigh. While duck is cooking, prepare Cumberland Sauce. Cool duck slightly.

Preheat broiler. Using a heavy cleaver or knife, cut duck into quarters. Place duck quarters, skin side up, in a shallow baking dish. Spoon Cumberland Sauce over duck. Broil for 4 to 5 minutes, or until sauce bubbles. Serve immediately with apples. ❖

Stuffed Turkey
Indyk Nadziewany

The strong liver flavor dominates this old-fashioned Polish stuffed turkey.

Makes 12 to 14 servings

1 (8- to 10-pound) turkey, thawed, if frozen
1 tablespoon plus ½ teaspoon salt
½ cup water
3 eggs, separated
2 tablespoons butter or margarine, at room temperature
1 turkey liver, minced
1½ tablespoons chopped fresh parsley
2 cups dry bread crumbs
¼ teaspoon freshly ground black pepper
¼ teaspoon ground cloves
¼ teaspoon ground nutmeg
¼ cup raisins
½ cup butter or margarine, melted
Red wine (optional)

Preheat oven to 325°F (165°C). Remove giblets and neck from turkey cavity; reserve for stock or soup. Rinse turkey under cold running water; pat dry with paper towels. Rub turkey, inside and out, with 1 tablespoon salt. Place turkey, breast side down, on a rack in a shallow roasting pan. Pour water into roasting pan.

In a medium bowl, beat egg yolks and 2 tablespoons butter until pale and creamy. Add liver, parsley, bread crumbs, ½ teaspoon salt, pepper, cloves, nutmeg, and raisins. In a medium bowl, beat egg whites until stiff peaks form; fold into egg yolk mixture.

Spoon crumb mixture into turkey cavity. Roast for 3½ to 4 hours, or until juices run clear when a knife is inserted between breast and thigh. Baste with melted butter every 20 minutes. Place turkey on a large platter. Cover with foil and let stand for 20 to 30 minutes before carving. If desired, pour pan juices into a small saucepan. Add wine (if using). Cook over medium heat, stirring constantly, 3 to 4 minutes. Spoon cooked juices over turkey slices and stuffing. ❦

Normandy Turkey

Indyk po Normandzku

Combining butter-basted turkey and aromatic Polish white sausage creates a special dinner.

Makes 8 to 10 servings

1 (8- to 8½-pound) turkey, thawed, if frozen
1 tablespoon salt
½ teaspoon freshly ground black pepper
10 small apples, peeled
½ cup butter or margarine, melted
2 tablespoons Cognac
1 cup Chicken Broth, page 35, or bouillon
1½ pounds Polish white sausage or fresh Polish sausage

Preheat oven to 350°F (175°C). Remove giblets and neck from turkey cavity; reserve for stock or soup. Rinse turkey under cold running water; pat dry with paper towels. Rub turkey, inside and out, with salt and pepper. Place turkey on a rack, breast side down, in a shallow roasting pan. Arrange peeled apples in turkey cavity.

In a small bowl, combine butter and Cognac. Pour broth into roasting pan. Roast turkey for 2 hours, basting every 15 minutes with Cognac mixture. Twist sausage into small links. Prick each link with a fork to let juices escape during cooking. After 2 hours cooking, place sausage links around turkey on bottom of roasting pan. Roast turkey and sausage for 30 minutes to 1 hour, or until juices run clear when a knife is inserted between breast and thigh.

Place turkey on a large platter. Keep sausage warm in oven. Cover turkey with foil and let stand for 20 to 30 minutes before carving. Before carving, arrange warm sausage links around turkey on platter. ❖

Spinach Omelet

Omlet ze Szpinakiem

The sweet red pepper sauce gives this omelet a special taste dimension.

Makes 1 serving

2 tablespoons plus 1 teaspoon butter or margarine

1 clove garlic, minced

½ pickled sweet red pepper or pimiento, sliced

1 tablespoon chopped fresh parsley

1 small tomato, chopped

½ teaspoon olive oil

½ cup chopped fresh spinach

2 eggs

1 tablespoon cold water

½ teaspoon salt

⅛ teaspoon ground white pepper

Melt 1 tablespoon of the butter in a small skillet over medium-low heat. Add garlic, red pepper, parsley, and tomato. Sauté for 3 to 4 minutes. Remove from heat; keep warm in oven.

Heat oil and 1 teaspoon butter in a small skillet over low heat. Add spinach. Sauté for 4 to 5 minutes.

In a medium bowl, beat eggs, water, salt, and white pepper. Melt the remaining 1 tablespoon butter in a medium skillet over medium-low heat. Pour egg mixture into skillet. Using a spatula, lift edges of eggs when they set. When eggs are half set, sprinkle spinach over half of omelet. Cook until eggs are almost set, freeing omelet from skillet bottom with spatula. Carefully fold omelet in half with spatula. Cook for 1 minute. Turn omelet over; cook for 1 minute. Serve immediately with red pepper mixture over omelet. ❖

Omelet with Peas

Omlet z Groszkiem

Surprise your guests with this delicious and unusual dish.

Makes 4 servings

Dill Sauce with Sour Cream, page 70
(optional)

1 cup fresh or frozen green peas

¼ cup plus 1 teaspoon butter or margarine

1 small onion, chopped

8 eggs

3 tablespoons half-and-half or milk

1 teaspoon salt

¼ teaspoon freshly ground black pepper

Prepare Dill Sauce with Sour Cream (if using); keep warm.

Place peas and 1 tablespoon of the butter in a small saucepan. Add enough salted water to cover. Bring to a boil over medium-high heat. Reduce heat to low. Cover and simmer until tender, 6 to 7 minutes. Drain.

Melt the 1 teaspoon butter in a small skillet over medium heat. Add onion; sauté until tender. Stir onion into peas. Place eggs, half-and-half, salt, and pepper in a medium bowl. Beat lightly with a fork until combined.

Melt the remaining 3 tablespoons butter in a large skillet over medium heat. Pour egg mixture into skillet. Using a spatula, lift edges of eggs when they set. When eggs are half set, sprinkle peas and onion over half of omelet. Cook until eggs are almost set, freeing omelet from skillet bottom with spatula. Carefully fold omelet in half with spatula. Cook for 1 minute. Turn omelet over; cook for 1 minute. Serve immediately with warm dill sauce (if using).❧

Bull's-Eye Eggs

Wolowe Oczy Jajka

This is a creative way to use common ingredients in a tasty and attractive dish.

Makes 4 servings

4 slices white bread

Butter or margarine, at room temperature

4 eggs

2 tablespoons half-and-half

Salt

Freshly ground black pepper

⅓ cup shredded sharp Cheddar cheese
(1½ ounces)

Finely chopped parsley

Preheat oven to 325°F (165°C). Lightly grease a large, shallow baking dish. Cut out a 2½-inch circle from center of each bread slice, leaving crust intact. Discard bread circles or reserve for another use. Lightly spread butter on 1 side of each bread piece. Heat a large skillet over medium heat. Add bread, buttered side down. Cook until lightly browned. Turn bread over; cook for 1 minute. Remove from skillet.

Place each bread piece in greased baking dish. Break 1 egg into each bread crust. Drizzle 1½ teaspoons half-and-half over each egg. Season with salt and pepper to taste. Top bread crusts with cheese. Bake for 15 to 20 minutes, or until egg whites set. Garnish with parsley. ❖

Cut each bacon slice into thirds. In a small skillet, fry bacon over medium heat until crisp. Drain on paper towels.

Cut each tomato into 8 wedges. Cut wedges in half crosswise. Melt butter in a medium skillet over medium heat. Add tomatoes, garlic, salt, and pepper; sauté, stirring gently, until tomatoes are cooked but not too soft, 2 to 3 minutes.

Add bacon; sauté for 1 minute. Add eggs; cook, gently stirring, over medium-low heat until cooked as desired. Place in a serving dish. Garnish with chives. ❖

Farmer's Eggs
Jajecznica Gospodarska

Some brave farmers use two or three times the amount of recommended pepper.

Makes 4 servings

½ pound bacon slices

2 medium tomatoes, peeled

1½ tablespoons butter or margarine

2 cloves garlic, crushed

½ teaspoon salt

¼ teaspoon freshly ground black pepper

6 eggs, beaten

2 tablespoons chopped fresh chives

Shirred Eggs
Pieczone Jajka

Cooked to perfection, these baked eggs have soft yolks and lightly set whites.

Makes 1 serving

2 tablespoons half-and-half

2 tablespoons minced ham

2 eggs

Salt

Freshly ground black pepper

Pinch chopped fresh parsley

Preheat oven to 325°F (165°C). Rub a ramekin or small round baking dish with butter, margarine, or olive oil. Place half-and-half and ham in buttered dish. Break eggs into dish. Sprinkle with salt and pepper. Garnish with parsley. Bake for 15 to 20 minutes, or until egg whites are set. Serve immediately. ⁂

Egg Cutlets

Kotlety z Jaj

In Poland, this dish is prepared as a flavorful substitute for meat.

Makes 10 cutlets

Mushroom Sauce, page 86
4 hard-cooked eggs
1 large stale hard roll
½ cup milk
2 tablespoons chopped fresh chives
¼ cup butter or margarine, at room temperature
1 egg
¾ teaspoon salt
¼ teaspoon freshly ground black pepper
About ½ cup dry bread crumbs

Prepare Mushroom Sauce; keep warm.

Using a grinder, grind hard-cooked eggs or finely chop. Cut roll in half; soak both halves in a small bowl with milk. Squeeze excess milk from roll. Discard milk.

In a medium bowl, combine chives and 1 tablespoon of the butter. Add ground eggs, raw egg, salt, pepper, and roll.

On a flat work surface, spread out ¼ cup of the bread crumbs evenly over about an 8 × 5-inch area. Place egg mixture on center of bread crumbs. Carefully shape a loaf about 10 × 3 inches and 1½ inches thick. Press bread crumbs evenly into the surface. Let stand at room temperature for 5 minutes. With a sharp knife, cut crosswise into 1-inch slices. Cover both sides of slices with remaining ¼ cup bread crumbs.

Melt the remaining 3 tablespoons butter in a large skillet over medium heat. Add egg cutlets; cook until both sides are browned, 1½ to 2 minutes on each side. Serve hot with Mushroom Sauce. ⁂

Pork

Imagine going back centuries in Poland, to a place where a band of disheveled hunters gather around a simmering pot full of aromatic ingredients. If you could listen to the hunters, you'd hear them tell exciting, animated stories of the chase, while they patiently waited long into the night for the pot's contents to cook to perfection.

Nine out of ten times, they were preparing *Bigos*. Bigos, or Hunter's Stew, is the most traditional of all Polish dishes. Even today it is still prepared after deer, bear, and wild boar hunts, using meat from the quarry. This is combined with pork, beef, kielbasa, sauerkraut, and other ingredients that blend in true harmony.

Bigos is included in this chapter because pork is still the main meat ingredient. Bigos is a dish that improves with age. In fact, it was common for hunters to simmer Bigos for several days, while celebrating the end of a hunting season or other major event. Bigos is only one of the many ways pork is featured in Polish cuisine. More people in Poland raise hogs or pigs than steers. A typical village family might keep three or four hogs per year, feeding them grain, vegetables, or table scraps. And hogs don't need large fields to graze in. Because pork is more readily available than beef, it finds its way into a larger variety of dishes.

Another special recipe is Vienna Pork Rolls, in which thick slices of pork loin are tenderized and salted. Then they're rolled up with a delightful filling of sautéed chopped ham and sour cream seasoned with thyme and garlic.

The most common pork dish is the simple, no-frill cutlet, tenderized boneless loin slices, breaded and sautéed until golden, sometimes with a surprising addition of a thin slice of Gouda, mozzarella, or provolone cheese.

From cutlets on, the pork pieces get smaller. In Bialystok Pork, they're slender strips sautéed with sliced mushrooms, onion, and green pepper, seasoned with the Polish substitute for soy sauce—Maggi seasoning—and sprinkled with ground ginger.

PORK AND LAMB

Another traditional way to prepare pork is to smoke it. Smoked pork loin is usually eaten cold, sliced for the appetizer tray, or used as a filling for sandwiches.

When my husband and I were married in Poland, the morning after our farmhouse reception, he helped my father return borrowed tables and chairs to our neighbors. After hauling a particularly heavy wood table into the thatched roof home of its owner—a wrinkled, toothless bachelor in his 70s, my husband was offered what he thought was a square piece of cheese, along with a shot of Polish spiritus or vodka.

My husband popped the "cheese" into his mouth, only to discover that in truth, it was a chunk of bacon fat. For one time the spiritus came in handy! Among the older generation in Poland, plain smoked bacon fat is considered a delicacy.

Lamb

Lamb is not as important to the Polish diet as it was years ago, when sheep were often raised for their wool. Yet the taste for lamb lingers on in many of the older segments of the population.

Lamb is a tender meat with a distinctive flavor all its own. The meat itself is covered with a thin membrane that feels like paper and is called the *fell*. The fell is generally removed before cooking.

An old standby, Lamb Cutlet, is flavored with ground sweet paprika and garlic, then simmered until tender in cooking juices of broth, butter or margarine, and onions.

Roast Lamb is begun by wrapping a boneless lamb roast with vinegar-soaked cheesecloth, then refrigerating the roast. A later stop finds slivers of garlic inserted in narrow slits cut throughout the roast's surface before the meat is browned and cooked.

Grits with Ham

Kasza z Szynka

Grits help make inexpensive and popular dishes; they're often served two or three times a week in Polish households, alternated with sides of potatoes or rice.

Makes 6 to 8 servings

3 tablespoons butter or margarine

1 medium onion, finely chopped

3 cups cooked grits, prepared according to package directions

1 teaspoon salt

¼ teaspoon freshly ground black pepper

¼ teaspoon ground cayenne pepper

3 eggs, beaten with a fork

1 cup grated Cheddar cheese (4 ounces)

2 cups diced cooked ham or crumbled cooked bacon

¼ cup chopped fresh parsley

Preheat oven to 325°F (165°C). Melt 2 tablespoons of the butter in a medium skillet over medium-high heat. Add onion; sauté until tender with dark brown bits. Grease a large casserole with remaining 1 tablespoon butter. Add grits, onion, and cooking juices, salt, black pepper, cayenne, eggs, cheese, ham, and parsley. Bake grits for 1½ hours, or until casserole is set. Serve hot.

Polish Spareribs

Zeberka po Polsku

Pork spareribs are widely available and very popular in Poland because many families raise their own pigs.

Makes 4 to 6 servings

1 cup all-purpose flour

3½ pounds pork spareribs, cut in 2-rib pieces

2 tablespoons vegetable oil

1 medium onion, finely chopped

2 garlic cloves, crushed

3 tablespoons tomato puree

2 tablespoons chili sauce

2 tablespoons red wine

Pinch ground cloves

½ teaspoon brown sugar

2½ cups beef broth

2 tablespoons cornstarch

⅓ cup water

Preheat oven to 350°F (175°C). Place flour in a large bowl. Toss ribs in flour, lightly coating the ribs. In a large skillet, heat oil over medium-high heat. Add ribs and cook until browned on both sides, turning. Transfer ribs to a roasting pan.

Add onion to the same skillet and sauté over medium heat until onion is tender. In a medium bowl, mix together garlic, tomato puree, chili sauce, wine, cloves, brown sugar, and broth. Pour over ribs. Cover and bake for 30 minutes. Uncover and bake for 30 minutes, or until ribs are tender. Transfer ribs to a serving platter. In a small bowl, blend cornstarch and water. Strain rib cooking sauce into a saucepan and stir in cornstarch mixture. Bring to a boil and cook, stirring constantly until sauce thickens. Spoon hot sauce over ribs.

Baked Pork Loin with Apples

Pieczony Schab z Jablkami.

Use one red apple and one green apple for a pleasing visual effect for this popular recipe.

Makes 6 (2-slice) servings

1 teaspoon salt
1 teaspoon freshly ground black pepper
1 teaspoon ground thyme
1 clove garlic, crushed
1 (4-pound) fresh boneless pork loin
2 tablespoons vegetable oil
2 apples, cored, not peeled (1 red, 1 green)
1 cup red wine
2 tablespoons cornstarch
¼ cup water
1 cup Chicken Broth, page 35

Preheat oven to 325°F (165°C). Lightly grease a large shallow baking pan. In a small bowl, mix salt, pepper, thyme, and garlic. Pat pork loin dry. Rub with salt mixture. Heat oil in a large skillet over medium-high heat. Add pork and sauté pork until all sides are browned. Remove pork from heat; let cool slightly. With a sharp knife, slice pockets crosswise into the pork from the top surface down three-fourths of the way through the loin. Make 12 evenly spaced pockets from one end of the loin to the other. Slice each apple into 6 circular pieces, horizontally from the top of each cored apple to the bottom. Insert each apple slice, alternating red and green apple slices, into the loin pockets.

Place loin in prepared baking pan. Roast, uncovered, for 1½ hours. Drizzle 1 cup red wine over roast. Cook for 30 minutes, or until desired level of doneness is reached. Transfer roast to a serving platter. Carefully slice roast so each piece contains a pocket having one apple slice. In a small bowl, blend cornstarch and water. Strain rib cooking sauce into a saucepan and stir in cornstarch mixture and broth. (If there is not enough cooking liquid and broth to make 2 cups, add additional to make 2 cups.) Bring to a boil and cook, stirring constantly until sauce thickens. Spoon hot sauce over sliced roast.

Polish White Sausage Bake

Biala Kielbasa Zapiekana

Fresh white Polish sausage can typically be found in ethnic markets and specialty butcher stores; it's a raw sausage that needs to be thoroughly cooked before being eaten.

Makes 4 to 6 servings

2 pounds fresh white Polish sausage, cut into 4-inch pieces
2 tablespoons vegetable oil
2 medium onions, each cut in 8 wedges
1 large green bell pepper, cut in large pieces
1 large red bell pepper, cut in large pieces
½ pound fresh mushrooms, sliced
1 cup Chicken Broth, page 35

Preheat oven to 325°F (165°C). Place sausage in a large saucepan; add enough water to cover. Cook, uncovered, over medium-low heat until water evaporates. Add oil. Increase heat to medium. Cook for 10 minutes, occasionally turning sausage pieces until all sides are browned. Add onions, bell peppers, and mushrooms. Cook over medium heat for 5 minutes, stirring several times. Transfer cooked sausage, vegetables, and pan juices into a large casserole. Add chicken broth. Cook, covered, for 1 hour. Serve hot.

Bialystok Pork

Przysmak Bialostocki

This recipe is a favorite of all three of my brothers.

Makes 4 to 6 servings

2 tablespoons butter or margarine
1 pound fresh mushrooms, sliced
2 pounds lean boneless pork
2 tablespoons vegetable oil
1 medium onion, chopped
1 small green bell pepper, chopped
2 tablespoons Maggi seasoning
1 teaspoon ground ginger
Cooked rice (optional)

Melt butter in a large skillet over medium heat. Add mushrooms; sauté until tender. Remove from heat.

Slice pork in ½-inch-thick strips, about 3½ inches long. Heat oil in a large skillet over medium heat. Add pork strips; sauté until evenly browned. Remove pork from skillet. Add onion and bell pepper to pork drippings; sauté until tender. Return pork to skillet. Add mushrooms, Maggi seasoning, and ginger. Cook, uncovered, over low heat until cooked through, 20 minutes, stirring occasionally. Serve over cooked rice (if using).

Stuffed Cabbage

Golabki

Worldwide, this is one of the most popular and best-known Polish dishes.

Makes 10 to 12 servings

1 (3-pound) head green cabbage

¼ cup butter or margarine

1 small onion, chopped

1 pound lean ground beef

1½ pounds lean ground pork

1½ cups cooked long-grain white rice

1 teaspoon salt

¼ teaspoon freshly ground black pepper

3½ cups Beef Broth, page 34, or bouillon

1 (6-ounce) can tomato paste

2 tablespoons all-purpose flour

With a sharp knife, remove core from cabbage. Carefully remove wilted or decayed outer cabbage leaves; discard. In a large saucepan, bring enough salted water to a boil to cover cabbage. Immerse cabbage in boiling water. Cook over medium-high heat for 5 to 7 minutes. With fork or tongs, gently remove leaves as they become tender. Drain well; let cool. Trim main leaf stems.

Preheat oven to 325°F (165°C). Melt 1 tablespoon of the butter in a small skillet over medium heat. Add onion; sauté until golden brown.

In a large bowl, combine onion, beef, pork, rice, salt, and pepper. Spread a cabbage leaf flat. Depending on leaf size, place 2 to 3 tablespoons filling on cabbage leaf near base. Fold bottom of leaf over filling, then fold sides toward center. Roll tightly. Repeat with remaining filling and cabbage leaves. Heat 1 tablespoon butter or margarine in a large skillet over medium heat. Place filled cabbage leaves, seam side down, in skillet. Cook until browned, 8 to 10 minutes, turning once with a spatula. Arrange cabbage rolls, seam side down, in a medium roasting pan.

Add 3 cups of the broth. In a small bowl, combine the remaining ½ cup broth and tomato paste. Pour over stuffed cabbage. Cover and bake 40 minutes or until fork-tender.

Melt the remaining 2 tablespoons butter in a small skillet over medium heat. Stir flour into butter until smooth. Cook, stirring, until golden brown. Ladle 1 cup broth from stuffed cabbage into flour mixture; blend. Pour mixture over stuffed cabbage. Bake, uncovered, until liquid bubbles and thickens slightly. Place stuffed cabbage on a large platter. Pour pan juices into a serving bowl. Serve hot with pan juices. ❧

Baked Pork Loin

Pieczona Poledwica Wieprzowa

In Poland, apples and pork often find their way into the same dishes.

Makes 6 to 8 servings

1 teaspoon salt

1 teaspoon freshly ground black pepper

¼ teaspoon ground marjoram

1 (4-pound) bone-in pork loin roast

All-purpose flour

3 tablespoons vegetable oil

2 medium onions, chopped

3 medium tart apples, peeled, shredded

1 cup water

Combine salt, pepper, and marjoram in a small bowl. Pat roast dry. Rub roast with salt mixture. Let stand for 15 minutes. Sprinkle roast with flour until evenly coated.

Preheat oven to 325°F (165°C). Heat oil in a large skillet over medium-high heat. Add roast; cook until browned on all sides. Place roast in a deep baking dish. Add onions to pan juices in skillet; sauté over medium heat until tender. Remove from heat. Stir apples into onions; spoon mixture over roast. Add water to bottom of baking dish.

Roast, uncovered, for 2 to 2½ hours, or until tender. Baste every 20 minutes, adding enough water to make sure at least 1 cup cooking juices

remains in baking dish throughout cooking time. When done, remove roast and strain cooking juices. Slice roast and serve hot with cooking juices on the side. ❧

Boneless Pork Loin

Schab Pieczony

In Poland, this cut of meat is usually saved for the holidays.

Makes 6 servings

1 (3-pound) boneless pork loin roast

5 cloves garlic, crushed

1 tablespoon salt

2 tablespoons vegetable oil

½ teaspoon freshly ground black pepper

3 medium onions, thinly sliced

½ cup Meat Broth, page 33, or bouillon

Pat roast dry. Combine garlic and salt in a small bowl. Rub roast with garlic mixture. Let stand for 15 minutes. Heat oil in a large deep skillet over medium-high heat. Add roast; cook until browned on all sides. Reduce heat to low. Sprinkle pepper over roast. Arrange onion slices on top of roast. Gently drizzle broth over onions. Cover and simmer for 2½ hours, or until tender, basting with cooking juices every 15 minutes, adding water if needed. To serve, slice and spoon cooked onions and juices over roast.

Variation

Substitute ½ teaspoon ground marjoram for pepper and 1 pound peeled, sliced tart apples for onions. Serve as above. ❧

Wild-Pork Roast

Dzika Pieczeń Wieprzowa

This recipe was developed in the seventeenth century using wild boar.

Makes 6 servings

1½ cups white wine

Juice of 1 lemon

10 black peppercorns

2 whole cloves

1 bay leaf

¼ teaspoon ground marjoram

1 (3-pound) boneless pork loin roast

3 medium onions

Salt

2 tablespoons vegetable oil

1 cup Chicken Broth, page 35, or bouillon

1 tablespoon jam, such as currant, cherry, or raspberry

1 tablespoon all-purpose flour

In a medium saucepan, combine wine, lemon juice, peppercorns, cloves, bay leaf, and marjoram. Bring to a boil over medium heat. Place pork loin in a deep, narrow nonmetallic baking dish. Slice 2 of the onions and arrange slices over pork. Pour wine marinade over meat and onions. Cover with plastic wrap or foil. Refrigerate for 2 to 3 days, turning roast twice per day.

Preheat oven to 325°F (165°C). Remove roast from marinade; reserve marinade. Pat roast dry. Rub with salt. Heat oil in a medium skillet over medium-high heat. Cook roast until brown on all sides. Place roast in a deep, narrow baking dish.

Roast, covered with a tight-fitting lid, for 30 minutes. Slice remaining onion and arrange slices over pork. Roast, covered, for 2 hours.

Strain marinade into a medium bowl. In a small bowl, combine broth, jam, and flour. Stir into marinade. Pour marinade mixture over pork. Roast, uncovered, for 20 to 30 minutes, or until tender. Slice pork; ladle sauce over each portion. ❧

Vienna Pork Rolls

Wiedenskie Sznycle

Here's a unique way to prepare pork chops.

Makes 4 servings

4 (1½-inch-thick) boneless pork loin slices

½ teaspoon salt

3 tablespoons butter or margarine

1 cup chopped cooked ham

6 tablespoons sour cream

¼ teaspoon ground thyme

2 cloves garlic, crushed

1 egg yolk

1 large onion, sliced

1 cup Meat Broth, page 33, or bouillon

1 tablespoon all-purpose flour

Place pork slices between plastic wrap. Using a meat mallet, pound pork slices to ovals approximately ½ inch thick. Rub both sides of pork pieces with salt.

Melt 1 tablespoon of the butter in a medium skillet over medium heat. Add ham; sauté, stirring, until browned. Reduce heat to low. Stir 3 tablespoons of the sour cream, thyme, and garlic into ham. Simmer for 10 minutes; do not boil. Let cool. Blend in egg yolk.

Arrange pork pieces on a flat surface. Place one-fourth of the ham mixture on each pork piece. Roll up jelly-roll style; tie with string.

Melt the remaining 2 tablespoons butter in a large skillet over medium heat. Add onion; sauté until tender. Remove onion from skillet; set aside. Place filled pork rolls in onion pan juices. Sauté over medium heat until browned on all sides. Return onion to skillet. Add broth. Cover with a tight-fitting lid; simmer over low heat until tender, 1 hour, turning occasionally. Remove pork rolls from skillet; keep warm.

In a small bowl, blend remaining 3 tablespoons sour cream and flour. Gently stir into cooking juices. Simmer until slightly thickened, 10 minutes; do not boil. Serve rolls hot with sauce.

Pork and Cheese Cutlets

Kotlety Schabowe z Serem

The cheese in this recipe will pleasantly surprise your dinner guests.

Makes 6 servings

2 pounds boneless pork loin, cut in 10 to 12 (½-inch-thick) slices
Salt
Freshly ground black pepper
10 to 12 (3-inch-square) thin slices Gouda, mozzarella, or provolone cheese
½ cup all-purpose flour
2 eggs, beaten
½ cup dry bread crumbs
2 tablespoons butter or margarine

Place pork pieces between 2 pieces of plastic wrap. Using a meat mallet, pound each side until pork pieces are about ¼ to ⅜ inch thick. Season pork pieces with salt and pepper.

Preheat oven to 350°F (175°C). Place 1 cheese slice on each piece of pork. Pat cheese firmly onto pork. Place flour, eggs, and bread crumbs in separate shallow dishes. Dip pork in flour, being careful to cover both sides, including cheese. Shake off excess. Dip each piece in egg, then in bread crumbs. Press bread crumbs evenly onto pork and cheese.

Melt butter in a large skillet over medium heat. Add cutlets, cheese side up; cook until browned on both sides, 7 to 10 minutes. Grease a large baking dish. Arrange cutlets, cheese side up, in dish so pieces do not touch each other. Bake, uncovered, for 20 minutes, or until tender. ✤

Pork Cutlets

Kotlety Schabowe

This is a simple-to-make, tasty, no-waste main dish.

Makes 6 servings

6 thick pork loin rib chops
¾ cup all-purpose flour
1 teaspoon salt
½ teaspoon freshly ground black pepper
½ teaspoon ground sweet paprika
2 eggs, beaten
1 cup dry bread crumbs
⅓ cup vegetable oil

Bone pork chops. Trim excess fat from meat. Score 1-inch cuts at 3 places on each pork chop edge to prevent curling while cooking. Place pork pieces between 2 pieces of plastic wrap. Using a meat mallet, pound 5 times on each side, or until pork pieces are about ½ inch thick.

Combine flour, salt, pepper, and paprika in a shallow dish. Place eggs and bread crumbs in separate shallow dishes. Dip pork pieces in flour mixture, then dip in egg and bread crumbs, pressing bread crumbs evenly onto pork. Place breaded pork pieces on a rack. Let stand for 15 minutes.

Heat oil in a large skillet over medium-low heat. Add pork cutlets. Cook, turning occasionally, until cooked through, 20 minutes.

Hash Polish Style

Zapiekanka

The combination of sour cream and mushrooms contrasts nicely with pork and potato flavors.

Makes 8 servings

½ ounces dried mushrooms

2½ cups water

3 pounds baking potatoes, peeled, sliced

1 teaspoon salt

2 tablespoons butter or margarine

1 pound pork strips (¼ inch thick, 1 inch long)

2 medium onions, chopped

⅛ teaspoon freshly ground black pepper

1 teaspoon chopped fresh parsley

½ pint sour cream (1 cup)

1 tablespoon all-purpose flour

Wash mushrooms; place in a small saucepan. Add the water. Cover; simmer over low heat until rehydrated, 25 to 30 minutes. Drain; reserve liquid. Let mushrooms cool.

Place potatoes and salt in a large saucepan; cover with water. Bring to a boil; cook until tender. Drain potatoes; set aside.

Melt butter in a large skillet over medium-low heat. Add pork strips and onions; sauté until pork browns and onions are tender, about 30 minutes. Add ⅔ cup reserved mushroom liquid. Reduce heat to low. Simmer, uncovered, for 5 minutes. Chop mushrooms. Stir mushrooms, pepper, and parsley into pork mixture. Simmer for 5 minutes.

Preheat oven to 350°F (175°C). Grease a 9-inch-square baking dish. Arrange one-third of the potatoes evenly on bottom of greased dish. Cover with half of the pork mixture, pat into an even layer. In a small bowl, combine sour cream, flour, and remaining mushroom liquid. Pour one-third of the sour cream mixture over pork layer. Add another layer of one-third of the potatoes. Top with the remaining pork. Spread with half of the remaining sour cream mixture. Layer remaining potatoes over sour cream mixture. Spread with remaining sour cream mixture. Smooth surface with a spoon. Bake, uncovered, for 40 minutes, or until top layer of sour cream sets and turns a dull, pale brown.

Spareribs Polish Style

Zeberka po Polsku

For preparation ease, have your butcher cut the ribs into serving-size pieces.

Makes 4 servings

¼ cup all-purpose flour

2 pounds pork spareribs, cut in pieces

2 tablespoons vegetable oil

4 medium onions, sliced

1 (6-ounce) can tomato paste

2 cups Beef Broth, page 34; Chicken Broth, page 35; or bouillon

1 teaspoon salt

½ teaspoon freshly ground black pepper

Place flour in a shallow dish. Roll spareribs in flour until evenly coated. Heat oil in a large skillet over medium heat. Add ribs; cook until evenly browned, 20 to 30 minutes. Remove ribs from skillet. Place on a plate; set aside.

Add onions to skillet; sauté until tender. Return ribs to skillet. In a small bowl, combine tomato paste and broth. Gently stir tomato mixture into rib mixture. Season with salt and pepper. Cover and simmer until tender, 40 minutes.

Variation
Preheat oven to 350°F (175°C). Prepare recipe as above through sautéing onions. Place spareribs in a shallow baking dish. Top with onions, tomato paste mixture, and seasonings. Cover and bake for 45 minutes, or until tender. ❧

Beer Sausage

Kielbasa w Piwnym Sosie

Polish sausage fixed a delightfully Polish way.

Makes 6 servings

3 pounds Polish sausage

1 (12-ounce) can or bottle light beer

1½ cups water

2 large onions, chopped

1 tablespoon butter or margarine

1 tablespoon all-purpose flour

Juice from 1 lemon

1 teaspoon sugar

½ teaspoon salt

1 teaspoon Maggi seasoning

Chopped fresh parsley

Place sausage in a large saucepan. Add beer, water, and onions. Cover and cook over medium-high heat for 20 minutes. Remove sausage, place in a casserole, and keep warm in oven. Strain sausage stock into a medium saucepan. Press onions through a strainer with a wooden spoon.

Melt butter in a small skillet over low heat. Add flour, stirring until well blended. Cook, stirring, until mixture turns a golden color, 2 to 3 minutes. Remove from heat. Stir in 2 tablespoons strained stock. Add lemon juice, sugar, salt, and Maggi seasoning. Bring to a boil, stirring constantly. Combine with stock in saucepan; bring to a boil over medium heat. Cook, stirring, until slightly thickened. Pour sauce over sausage. Garnish with parsley. ❖

Pork and Vegetable Goulash

Gulasz Wieprzowy z Jarzynami

Instead of all pork, substitute half veal or beef.

Makes 6 servings

½ cup all-purpose flour

1 teaspoon salt

⅛ teaspoon freshly ground black pepper

1½ pounds lean pork, cut into 1-inch cubes

1 tablespoon butter or margarine

3½ cups Meat Broth, page 33, or bouillon

1 medium onion, chopped

½ cup shredded carrot

¼ cup shredded parsley root

½ cup chopped leek

½ cup chopped celery

3 medium tomatoes, peeled, quartered

Cooked rice or noodles

In a plastic bag, combine flour, salt, and pepper. Add pork cubes; shake until well coated.

Melt butter in a large skillet over medium-high heat. Add pork; sauté until evenly browned, 8 to 10 minutes. Add broth. Cover and simmer for 20 minutes.

Add onion, carrot, parsley root, leek, and celery. Cover; simmer until vegetables are tender, 30 minutes. Add tomatoes. Cover; simmer until tomatoes are cooked, 5 to 10 minutes. Serve hot over rice. ❖

Pork Patties

Kotlety Mielone

Serve these economical patties with Dill Sauce with Sour Cream, page 70, or Mushroom Sauce, page 86.

Makes 6 servings

¼ cup milk

1 large stale hard roll

1½ pounds lean ground pork

1 egg

3 tablespoons chopped fresh dill or 1 tablespoon dried

1 teaspoon salt

¼ teaspoon freshly ground black pepper

⅓ cup dry bread crumbs

¼ cup vegetable oil

½ cup Meat Broth, page 33, or bouillon

Place milk in a medium bowl. Break roll apart; add to milk. Soak until milk is absorbed. Blend in pork, egg, dill, salt, and pepper. On a flat surface, shape into 6 (1-inch-thick) patties.

Place bread crumbs in a shallow dish. Dip pork patties in bread crumbs, lightly pressing bread crumbs evenly onto pork.

Heat oil in a large skillet over medium heat. Add pork patties; sauté until both sides are browned, 10 to 12 minutes. Add broth to skillet. Reduce heat to low. Simmer, uncovered, for 10 to 12 minutes, turning once. Serve hot.

Scrambled Eggs and Smoked Pork Loin

Jajecznica z Wedzona Poledwica

Probably the most popular scrambled egg recipe, usually served with fresh hard rolls and butter.

Makes 4 servings

12 (¼-inch-thick) slices smoked pork loin

1 tablespoon butter or margarine

8 eggs

Cut pork into ½- to 1-inch pieces. Melt butter in a large skillet over medium-low heat. Add pork; sauté until lightly browned on both sides.

Break eggs into a medium bowl; beat lightly. With a fork, gently stir eggs into pork. Stir constantly so eggs will not stick. When eggs set but are still moist, remove from heat. Serve immediately.

Variations

Add ¼ cup chopped onion when sautéing pork.

Substitute 4 cups sliced Polish sausage, cooked and drained, or 4 cups sliced fresh mushrooms for smoked pork loin.

Hunter's Stew

Bigos

A harmonious blend of flavors, it is known as the Polish national dish.

Makes 12 to 14 servings

3 pounds sauerkraut

2 pounds ham with bone, pork spareribs, or pork rib roast

2 bay leaves

1 ounce dried mushrooms, chopped

20 black peppercorns

10 allspice berries

½ teaspoon salt

11 cups Beef Broth, page 34; bouillon; or water

2 pounds green cabbage, chopped like sauerkraut

2 tablespoons butter or margarine

1 pound Polish smoked sausage, cut into ½-inch cubes

1 pound Polish white sausage with garlic, cut into ½-inch cubes

1 pound bacon, cut into ½-inch cubes

Rinse sauerkraut with cold water; drain well. In a large stockpot, combine sauerkraut, meat, bay leaves, mushrooms, peppercorns, allspice, and salt. Add 6 cups of the broth. Cook, uncovered, over medium heat for 15 minutes. Cover and simmer over low heat for 45 minutes. Remove meat. Let meat cool.

Meanwhile, place cabbage in a large saucepan. Add remaining 5 cups broth. Bring to a boil. Cook, uncovered, over medium heat, until cabbage is tender, 1 hour. Add to sauerkraut mixture.

Bone cooked meat. Cut meat into ½-inch cubes. Melt butter in a large skillet. Add meat, smoked sausage, and white sausage. Sauté over medium heat until browned, 10 minutes. Add to sauerkraut mixture.

In same skillet, sauté bacon over medium heat until crisp. Drain bacon on paper towels. Add to sauerkraut mixture. Cover; cook over low heat for 1 hour or longer. Remove and discard bay leaves. Serve hot.

Tip

Use only meat with large bones, so bones can be removed easily. The secret of old-time Bigos is that it gets better as it's reheated on successive days, peaking at the sixth or seventh day. In between, store covered in the refrigerator and bring to a full boil before serving. ❧

Roast Lamb

Pieczen Barania

Cheesecloth soaked in white vinegar provides a custom marinade for this choice cut of lamb.

Makes 14 to 16 servings

1 (5½- to 6-pound) boneless lamb roast
½ cup white vinegar
Salt
8 cloves garlic, slivered
¼ cup all-purpose flour
½ to 1 cup water

Place lamb in a shallow baking dish. In a bowl, soak a large piece of cheesecloth in vinegar. Remove cheesecloth from bowl; do not squeeze out. Wrap lamb tightly with cheesecloth. Cover; refrigerate for up to 2 days. Rinse lamb with cold water. Pat dry with paper towels.

Preheat oven to 350°F (175°C). Lightly oil a small roasting pan. Sprinkle roast with salt. Using a sharp knife, cut small deep slits evenly spaced over roast. Insert garlic slivers in slits. Evenly sprinkle roast with flour. Place roast in oiled pan. Cook over medium heat until evenly browned. Add water to pan.

Roast, uncovered, for 3 hours, or until tender. Baste with cooking juices every 20 minutes, adding water as necessary.

Lamb Cutlets

Kotlety Baranie

The Poles' fondness for sweet paprika is reflected in yet another distinctive main dish.

Makes 6 to 9 servings

2½ to 3 pounds boneless lamb, cut in 1-inch-thick pieces
1 tablespoon ground sweet paprika
1½ teaspoons salt
1 tablespoon all-purpose flour
2 tablespoons vegetable oil
2 tablespoons butter or margarine
8 cloves garlic, crushed
2 medium onions, chopped
3 cups Chicken Broth, page 35, or bouillon
2 tablespoons cornstarch
¼ cup water

Place lamb pieces between plastic wrap. Using a meat mallet, pound lamb until ½ inch thick. Combine paprika, salt, and flour in a small bowl. Dip lamb pieces in paprika mixture. Let stand for 20 minutes.

Heat oil in a large, heavy skillet over medium heat. Add lamb; sauté until evenly browned. Melt butter in a medium skillet over medium heat. Add garlic and onions; sauté until tender. Add garlic and onions to lamb. Pour broth over lamb, garlic, and onions.

Cover and cook over medium-low heat until tender, 40 to 50 minutes, turning once. Remove lamb from skillet; place on a warm platter.

In a small bowl, blend cornstarch and water. Stir cornstarch mixture into cooking juices. Bring to a boil; cook, stirring, until thickened. To serve, ladle cooking juices over lamb.❖

Heat oil in a large skillet over medium heat. Add lamb; sauté until evenly browned. Add onions. Reduce heat to low. Sauté until onions become partially tender. Add broth. Cover and simmer for 35 minutes, stirring occasionally. Stir in tomato paste. Simmer until lamb is tender, 20 minutes. Stir reserved flour mixture into lamb and cooking juices. Bring to a boil over medium heat; cook, stirring, until thickened. Serve hot, over rice (if using). Garnish with parsley.❖

Simple Lamb Stew
Gulasz Barani

Really a lamb goulash.

Makes 6 servings

¼ cup all-purpose flour

1 teaspoon salt

¼ teaspoon ground sweet paprika

⅛ teaspoon freshly ground black pepper

2 pounds boneless lamb, cut in ¾-inch cubes

2 tablespoons vegetable oil

2 medium onions, quartered

1 cup Chicken Broth, page 35, or bouillon

1 cup tomato paste

Cooked rice (optional)

Chopped fresh parsley

Combine flour, salt, paprika, and pepper in a shallow dish. Roll lamb in flour mixture; reserve remaining flour mixture.

Fish

A late December tradition that still exists at my home in northeastern Poland unfolds when my father brings home several live carp from the market. Once home, he places the 3- to 4-pound fish in a tub filled with chilly well water that cleans every taint of silt or mud from the carp's system. Several days later, the still alive and healthy carp are passed into the care of my mother. She, however, is not so kind. She scales, dresses, and more often than not prepares them in a variety of dishes.

In addition to carp, another fish commonly found in Polish lakes and rivers is the barracuda-like northern pike. Pike is most often fried, stuffed, and baked, or simmered in a light broth.

One notable pike recipe is Stuffed Pike, in which the cavity of a 5- to 6-pound northern pike is filled with a stuffing of onions, celery, apples, mushrooms, croutons, and parsley mixed with eggs. It's flavored with white wine, lemon juice, and thyme.

Although carp and northern pike make up an important part of the Poles' nonmeat diet, for sheer volume, no fish can approach the popularity enjoyed by the common herring. In Poland you'll find herring of all sizes salted, pickled, and marinated in oil. They're prepared in hot dishes, fried in omelets, batter-dipped or breaded and deep-fried, or simmered in broth and onions.

FISH AND GAME

At least half the fish consumed in Poland is prepared as cold dishes. Several chilled fish snacks appear in the appetizer chapter. Look for other cold fish recipes in the salad chapter. Many main dishes are also prepared cold, such as Cold Fillets in Vegetable Sauce, in which chunks of sautéed fillets are sprinkled with lemon juice, then refrigerated overnight in a sauce of tomato, onion, celery, carrot, and parsley root.

Occasionally frozen cod, haddock, ocean perch, and other saltwater varieties are available in grocery stores in blocks of frozen fillets. These fillets are poached, boiled, steamed, fried, baked, and sometimes broiled.

Regarding whole fresh fish, only the largest are filleted because the Polish cook believes that filleting results in excessive waste of meat and flavor in the smaller catches.

One January in Poland, after my husband emerged from the forest with a creel of fresh perch that had been caught through the ice, he decided to scale, fillet, and fry them, Pennsylvania style, for my family. I'll never forget how my mother watched aghast as he carried out his plans, and how on the sly she salvaged the discarded heads and bones. Later she made a delicious broth that my husband enjoyed, none the wiser.

Rabbit

Rabbit is the most accessible game meat in Poland. Even though hunting licenses, and the licenses needed to own and carry firearms, are too expensive for the average Pole, rabbits still find their way onto the typical family table. Rabbits are so common in Poland, and so simple to catch in homemade snares, that even young boys are sent into the forest to catch Sunday's main dish.

Rabbit is a sweet meat that tastes much like chicken. It can be fried, braised, boiled, stewed, or used in practically any recipe that calls for chicken.

Young rabbits are most tender. Older rabbits tend to be tough and stringy. It's best to get rabbit in the fall or winter months, when the meat is generally at its peak.

If your rabbit will come from a hunter relative or friend, have it skinned and dressed as soon as possible after it's killed. Scent glands located under the front legs where they join the body should be removed to avoid tainting the meat.

Soak rabbit overnight in salted water and a few tablespoons of vinegar to reduce any strong wild game flavor that might be present. This is not necessary if using tame rabbit. ❧

Quick-Braised Salmon Fillet

Losos Duszony

This recipe results in a healthy, delicious entrée in less than 30 minutes, start to finish.

Makes 4 servings

 2 pounds fresh or thawed frozen salmon fillets, skin on, cut into serving-size pieces
 About ¼ cup vegetable oil
 2 tablespoons minced garlic
 Cayenne pepper
 2 tablespoons chopped fresh parsley
 ¼ cup dry bread crumbs
 About ½ cup Chicken Broth, page 35, or equivalent dried bouillon and water

Place salmon pieces, skin side down, on a work surface. Lightly rub top surfaces of salmon with 2 tablespoons of the oil. Sprinkle garlic, cayenne, parsley, and bread crumbs evenly over fish. Heat the remaining 2 tablespoons oil in a large nonstick skillet. Add salmon, skin side down. Sauté over medium-high heat until salmon pieces are cooked at least halfway through, 2 minutes. If salmon fillets are very thick, cover with a heatproof lid to assist cooking. When cooked at least halfway through, using a firm spatula, turn salmon pieces, being careful to lift skin from pan and turn with each piece of fish.

Add chicken broth to skillet and cook, uncovered, over medium-high heat until broth is almost evaporated and fish is opaque throughout and flakes easily with a fork, 2 minutes. Turn fish pieces one more time and cook for 1 minute over medium heat. Serve hot. ❧

Stuffed Pike

Szczupak Nadziewany

Trout, salmon, carp, or whitefish may also be prepared this way.

Makes 8 to 10 servings

1 teaspoon salt

½ teaspoon freshly ground black pepper

¼ teaspoon ground sweet paprika

1 (5- to 6-pound) dressed pike

½ cup butter or margarine

2 large onions, chopped

1 large celery root, shredded, or 3 celery stalks, chopped

3 medium apples, peeled, chopped

1½ tablespoons chopped fresh parsley

1 cup fresh mushrooms, minced

About 4½ cups croutons

1½ teaspoons sugar

½ teaspoon ground thyme

Juice of ½ lemon

3 eggs

About ⅔ cup white wine

3 tablespoons butter or margarine, melted

Combine salt, pepper, and paprika in a small bowl. Rub salt mixture evenly over fish cavity. Cover; refrigerate for 15 minutes.

Preheat oven to 350°F (175°C). Grease a 13 × 9-inch baking dish. Melt the ½ cup butter in a large skillet over medium heat. Add onions and celery root; sauté until tender. Reduce heat to low. Add apples, parsley, and mushrooms. Simmer, stirring, until mushrooms become tender; remove from heat. Add 4½ cups croutons, sugar, thyme, lemon juice, eggs, and wine. Stir to combine. If stuffing mixture is too dry, add a little wine; if too moist, add a few more croutons. Cool.

Loosely fill fish cavity with stuffing, allowing room for expansion during cooking. Place fish in greased dish. Bake for 35 to 45 minutes, or until fish is opaque throughout and flakes easily with a fork. Baste with the melted butter about every 10 minutes. Serve immediately. ⊰

Fish Croquettes

Krokiety Rybne

These tasty morsels will turn simple broth or bouillon into something special.

Makes about 30 fish croquettes

1½ pounds fresh or thawed frozen fish fillets, skinned

1½ slightly stale dinner rolls

1 cup milk

2 eggs

1 teaspoon salt

¼ teaspoon white pepper

1 tablespoon chopped fresh parsley

2 to 4 quarts Chicken Broth, page 35, or bouillon

Using a grinder, grind fish into a medium bowl. In a small bowl, soak rolls in milk until it is absorbed. With your hands, squeeze excess milk from rolls. Grind squeezed rolls; add to fish along with eggs, salt, white pepper, and parsley. Blend fish mixture. With wet hands, form walnut-size balls from fish mixture. Place each ball on a baking sheet.

In a large saucepan, bring 2 to 2½ quarts of the broth to a boil over high heat. Gently drop fish balls into boiling liquid; bring back to a boil. Reduce heat to medium. Cook, uncovered, until croquettes float, 8 to 10 minutes.

Cover with a tight-fitting lid. Cook for 5 to 7 minutes, or until a total of 15 minutes is reached. Remove croquettes with a slotted spoon; discard cooking liquid. Place croquettes on a platter. Bring remaining broth to a boil and serve with croquette (if desired).

Tip

If fish mixture is very soft, add enough dry bread crumbs to bring mixture to a proper handling consistency.

Mushroom-Topped Fish Fillets

Ryba Zapiekna z Pieczarkami

An elegant yet simple dish, perfect for entertaining.

Makes 4 to 6 servings

1½ tablespoons butter or margarine

½ pound fresh mushrooms, sliced

1½ pounds fresh fish fillets

Juice of ½ lemon

½ teaspoon salt

¼ cup sour cream

½ cup shredded sharp Cheddar cheese (2 ounces)

Sweet paprika

2 tablespoons dry bread crumbs

Melt butter in a medium skillet over medium heat. Add mushrooms; sauté until tender and liquid evaporates.

Preheat broiler. Grease a large, shallow baking dish. Arrange fillets in greased dish. Sprinkle with lemon juice and salt. Broil for 5 minutes. Spoon mushrooms over fillets. Spoon sour cream over mushrooms. Top with cheese, paprika to taste, and bread crumbs. Broil for 5 to 8 minutes, or until fish is opaque throughout and flakes easily with a fork. ❖

Broiled Fillets

Zapiekane Filety

Serve these tender fish fillets with boiled potatoes and Fisherman's Salad, page 62.

Makes 6 servings

6 freshwater fish fillets (about 2 pounds)

Juice of ½ lemon

Salt

Freshly ground black pepper

Dried Italian seasoning

2 tablespoons vegetable oil

2 tablespoons butter or margarine, at room temperature

2 tablespoons grated Parmesan cheese

⅓ cup sour cream

Arrange fillets, skin side down, in a shallow dish. Sprinkle with lemon juice, salt, pepper, and Italian seasoning to taste. Let stand for 15 minutes.

Preheat broiler. Lightly grease a baking dish. Heat oil in a large skillet over medium heat. Place fillets, skin side down, in skillet. Cook for 3 to 4 minutes. Turn and cook for 2 minutes.

Place fillets in greased dish, skin side down. Dab 1 teaspoon butter on each fillet, top with cheese. Broil fish for 2 minutes. Spread sour cream evenly over fillets. Broil for 5 minutes, or until fish is opaque throughout and flakes easily with a fork. ❖

Tartar Sauce

Sos Tatarski

Adding pickled mushrooms makes this tasty version of tartar sauce truly unique.

Makes about 1½ cups

1⅛ cups Mayonnaise, page 64, or other mayonnaise
2 medium dill pickles, peeled, diced
¼ cup pickled mushrooms, diced
1 teaspoon minced onion
1 teaspoon prepared mustard

Combine all ingredients in a medium bowl. Cover and refrigerate for 30 minutes before serving.

Fish in Aspic

Ryba w Galarecie

A cool, colorful fish dish, it's perfect to serve at a buffet or special luncheon.

Makes 6 to 8 servings

4 cups Vegetable Broth, page 35, or chicken bouillon
2 pounds dressed pike, carp, or trout
5 black peppercorns
2 bay leaves
10 capers
1½ tablespoons unflavored gelatin powder
3 tablespoons cold water
1 large carrot, thinly sliced
½ lemon, thinly sliced
4 hard-cooked eggs, cut in wedges
Fresh parsley sprigs
Fresh lettuce or spinach

Heat broth in a medium saucepan over low heat. Cut fish into 2-inch pieces. Add fish, peppercorns, bay leaves, and capers to hot broth. Simmer, partially covered, until fish is opaque throughout and flakes easily with a fork, 20 to 30 minutes. Remove fish from cooking liquid. Strain liquid into a medium bowl.

In a small bowl, dissolve gelatin in water. Stir into strained liquid; let cool slightly. Pour a thin layer of gelatin mixture into a deep,

2-quart casserole or 3-inch-deep loaf dish. Refrigerate until set.

Arrange a few carrot slices, lemon slices, egg wedges, and parsley over set gelatin; top with a small amount of gelatin mixture. Refrigerate until set. Arrange fish pieces over set gelatin. Gently pour remaining gelatin mixture over fish. Cover and refrigerate until set.

Line a large platter with fresh lettuce or spinach. To serve, dip casserole or loaf dish in hot water several seconds. Invert aspic onto lined platter. Serve chilled. ❧

Cold Fillets in Vegetable Sauce
Ryba na Zimno w Sosie Warzywnym

In Poland fresh carp is often used as the main ingredient in this tasty appetizer.

Makes 10 to 12 servings

¾ cup plus 2 tablespoons vegetable oil
½ teaspoon salt
2 small onions, minced
½ celery root, shredded
2 medium carrots, shredded
1 leek, thinly sliced
1 parsley root, shredded
3 tablespoons tomato paste
¼ cup Chicken Broth, page 35, or bouillon
⅛ teaspoon freshly ground black pepper
½ teaspoon sugar
1½ pounds fresh fish fillets, skinned
⅓ cup all-purpose flour
Juice of ½ lemon

In a medium saucepan, combine the ¾ cup oil, salt, onions, celery root, carrots, leek, and parsley root. Cook, uncovered, over medium-low heat until vegetables are tender, 15 to 20 minutes. In a small bowl, blend tomato paste and broth. Stir into vegetables. Cook for 15 minutes over medium-low heat, stirring occasionally. Season with pepper and sugar.

Meanwhile, cut fillets into 3-inch pieces.

Heat the 2 tablespoons oil in a large skillet over medium-high heat. Place flour in a shallow dish. Roll fish pieces in flour until evenly coated; shake off excess. Add fish pieces to skillet. Fry until fish is opaque throughout and flakes easily with a fork, 4 to 6 minutes on each side.

Carefully transfer fish to a medium baking dish. Sprinkle with lemon juice. Spoon cooked vegetable mixture over fish. Let cool. Cover and refrigerate overnight. Serve chilled. ❖

Roast Pheasant

Bezant Pinecone

The bacon slices ensure a moist, tender bird.

Makes 4 servings

1 (3½- to 4-pound) pheasant
Salt
Freshly ground black pepper
1 teaspoon ground allspice
7 thin slices bacon
1 cup Veal Broth, page 36, or Chicken Broth, page 35

Preheat oven to 375°F (190°C). Rub pheasant with salt, inside and out. Sprinkle pepper and allspice over top of pheasant breast. Wrap pheasant with bacon slices by stretching bacon around breast and securing with butcher's string. Place pheasant in a baking dish. Add broth. Bake, uncovered, for 40 minutes, or until tender. ❖

Braised Rabbit with Mushrooms

Duszony Zając z Pieczarkami

This is a scaled-down version for medium-size rabbits instead of 12- or 14-pound Polish hares.

Makes 4 servings

¼ cup plus 2 tablespoons butter or margarine
10 small pearl onions
1 (4- to 4½-pound) rabbit
2 teaspoons salt
1 tablespoon all-purpose flour
2 bay leaves
⅛ teaspoon ground thyme
6 black peppercorns
1 cup Chicken Broth, page 35, or Vegetable Broth, page 35
½ pound fresh mushrooms, sliced
2¼ cups dry red wine

Melt the ¼ cup butter in a large skillet over medium heat. Add onions; sauté until onions are tender. Remove onions from skillet; set aside in a small bowl.

Place rabbit in same skillet; sauté over medium heat until both sides are browned, 7 to 8 minutes on each side. Sprinkle salt and flour over rabbit. Add bay leaves, thyme, peppercorns, and broth to skillet. Cover with a tight-fitting lid. Simmer over low heat for 1 hour, turning rabbit several times. Add onions to rabbit.

Melt the 2 tablespoons butter or margarine in a medium skillet over medium heat. Add mushrooms; sauté until tender. Add to rabbit. Pour wine over rabbit. Cover and simmer until rabbit is tender, 25 minutes. Place rabbit on a warm serving platter. Spoon onions, mushrooms, and cooking juices over rabbit. Serve hot.

Baked Rabbit

Zajac

Although it takes a long time to prepare, this tasty recipe is really quite simple.

Makes 4 servings

    1 cup vinegar
    1 bay leaf
    10 black peppercorns
    1 (4- to 4½-pound) rabbit, cut up
    ¼ pound fresh bacon slices
    1 cup sour cream
    1 tablespoon all-purpose flour

Place vinegar, bay leaf, and peppercorns in a small saucepan. Bring to a boil over medium heat. Reduce heat to low. Simmer for 15 minutes. Let cool.

Place rabbit pieces in a shallow baking dish. Pour vinegar mixture over rabbit. Cover and refrigerate for 12 to 24 hours, turning occasionally.

Preheat oven to 350°F (175°C). Remove rabbit from marinade, reserving marinade. Pat rabbit dry with paper towels. Wrap rabbit pieces with bacon slices by stretching bacon around rabbit and securing with wooden picks. Return wrapped rabbit to marinade. Bake, uncovered, for 45 minutes, or until tender, turning once. Combine sour cream and flour in a small bowl. Spoon sour cream mixture over rabbit. Bake for 15 minutes.

Beef

In Poland, a strip, sirloin, or porterhouse steak used to be all but unheard of until a few years ago. Beef was available from time to time, but only in the poorest of cuts. The best steaks and roasts somehow seemed to find their way out of the country. Beef cuts that remained were roasts, lean cuts like flank steak and, once in a while, beef round plus ground beef and beef bones.

This is not to say that beef doesn't have its niche in Polish cooking. It has. Beef bones and scraps have flavored many a rich broth traditionally used as a base for important dishes like Flaki.

Ground beef is prepared into Beef Patties, and various fillings for pierogies and other recipes. When combined with ground pork, it rallies into a delicious Meat Loaf with Eggs.

Slices of lean beef often are tenderized with a meat mallet, then rolled jelly-roll style along with vegetable or other filling mixtures. The rolls are simmered in a flavorful beef broth thickened with a flour and butter or sour cream mixture.

Then there's a special, once-a-year roast beef, stuffed with a sweet red-onion filling in deep pockets, carved so each moist slice contains a flavorful helping of onions.

Beef liver—more available than beef—is usually sautéed with onion rings and simmered in wine.

BEEF AND VEAL

Veal

Veal is the third most common meat in Poland, far behind chicken and pork, and slightly ahead of beef. The Poles like its delicate, mild flavor, and the way it easily accepts the flavors of any herbs or seasonings it's cooked with. But the wise cook also knows that there's little marbling or fat in the young white to light-pink meat, and if not carefully watched, veal can easily be dried out during cooking.

Many families living on small or large farms, or even in homes on the outskirts of large towns and cities, own at least one milk cow. That being the case, there's usually one enterprising individual in the area who keeps several bulls that do little else than service all of the milk cows for miles around. The milk cows bear calves, which helps perpetuate their milk-producing abilities and also provides a source of fresh veal.

Veal in Poland is prepared in a manner similar to pork. Boneless slices of veal leg or loin are pounded with a meat mallet or flat side of a cleaver. They're braised, breaded, and sautéed, used for cutlets, or stuffed and rolled, as in Veal Rollups. Here, tenderized veal is seasoned, rolled up around slices of bacon, sautéed with onions, and simmered in a mixture of chicken broth, tomatoes, and seasoning thickened with sour cream and flour.

Pocket Veal Roast is a unique roast variation. A boneless veal roast is prepared by cutting pockets and inserting folded bacon slices in each pocket. Chopped zucchini arranged around the roast helps make the cooking juices something special to be strained and served hot over carved slices of moist, tender veal. ❖

Veal and Eggs
Cielecina z Jajkami

A mild-flavored breakfast dish, it is popular during the fall.

Makes 6 servings

¼ cup butter or margarine
3 cups chopped cooked veal
1 medium onion, chopped
2 cloves garlic, minced
1 teaspoon salt
¼ teaspoon freshly ground black pepper
8 eggs

Melt 2 tablespoons of the butter in a large skillet over medium heat. Add veal, onion, garlic, salt, and pepper; sauté until onions are tender. Add the remaining 2 tablespoons butter.

In a medium bowl, lightly beat eggs with a fork. Stir into veal mixture. Reduce heat to medium-low. Cook, gently stirring, until eggs set but are still moist. Remove from heat. Serve immediately.

Pocket Veal Roast
Pieczen z Cieleciny Nadziewana

The delicate flavor of veal complements the fresh taste of lemon and zucchini in this no-waste main dish.

Makes 6 to 8 servings

1 (3- to 3½-pound) boneless rolled veal shoulder or rump roast, tied with string
10 to 12 bacon slices
1 cup Chicken Broth, page 35, or bouillon
1 tablespoon butter or margarine, melted
Juice of ½ lemon
1 teaspoon salt
1 tablespoon freshly grated lemon peel
2 anchovy fillets, drained and minced
1 tablespoon dry bread crumbs
1 medium zucchini, chopped

Preheat oven to 350°F (175°C). With a sharp knife, cut 10 to 12 (2-inch) pockets in veal, evenly spaced over top and sides of roast. Insert 1 folded bacon slice in each pocket. Place veal on a rack in a roasting pan. Sprinkle top of veal with broth, butter, lemon juice, salt, lemon peel, and anchovies. Top with bread crumbs. Place zucchini around bottom of roast. Cover with a tight-fitting lid.

Roast for 1½ to 2 hours, or until tender. Remove roast and let stand, covered, for 15 minutes. Strain cooking juices into a serving bowl; reserve zucchini. Slice roast; arrange slices on a warm platter. Serve with cooking juices and zucchini.

Veal Paprika

Paprykarz Cielecy

A great way to spice up the mild flavor of veal, this is a good dish for company.

Makes 6 to 8 servings

2 to 2½ pounds veal

¼ cup plus 1 tablespoon all-purpose flour

2 tablespoons vegetable oil

2 large onions, minced

1 tablespoon ground sweet paprika

½ cup Chicken Broth, page 35, or bouillon

½ cup sour cream

1 teaspoon salt

Juice from ½ lemon

Hot cooked white rice

Cut veal into bite-size pieces. Place the ¼ cup flour and veal pieces in a heavy plastic bag; shake to coat with flour. Heat oil in a large skillet over medium heat. Add veal; sauté until browned on all sides. Add onions; sprinkle with paprika. Pour broth into skillet. Cover and cook over medium-low heat until veal is tender, 30 minutes, stirring occasionally.

In a small bowl, combine sour cream and the 1 tablespoon flour. Stir sour cream mixture into veal and cooking juices. Cook, stirring, until juices are slightly thickened; do not boil. Season with salt and lemon juice. Serve hot over rice.

Veal Rollups

Zrazy Cielece

These delicate rollups will provide your guests with a tasty, light dinner.

Makes 6 servings

2 to 2½ pounds boneless veal

Freshly ground black pepper

12 bacon slices

About 1½ tablespoons all-purpose flour

2 tablespoons vegetable oil

1 large onion, halved, sliced

1 cup Chicken Broth, page 35, or bouillon

8 medium tomatoes, peeled, sliced

1 teaspoon salt

½ teaspoon sugar

½ teaspoon ground sweet paprika

2 tablespoons all-purpose flour

3 tablespoons sour cream

Fresh chopped parsley

Cut veal into 12 (½-inch-thick) pieces; place between plastic wrap. Using a meat mallet, pound each piece until ⅛ inch thick. Sprinkle with pepper. Place 1 bacon slice on each piece of veal. Roll jelly-roll style. Secure with wooden picks. Evenly sprinkle veal rolls with flour.

Heat oil in a large skillet over medium heat. Add onion and veal rolls; sauté until browned on all sides.

Heat broth in a large saucepan. Add onion and veal rolls. Cover and simmer for 15 minutes. Add tomatoes, salt, ½ teaspoon pepper, sugar, and paprika. Cover and simmer for 20 minutes.

In a small bowl, combine flour and sour cream. Stir flour mixture into simmering veal rolls and cooking juices. Increase heat to medium. Cook, stirring, until slightly thickened. To serve, arrange veal rolls on a warm platter. Top with cooking juices. Garnish with parsley. Serve immediately.❧

Pan-Braised Veal

Cielecina Duszona

Serve this dish with boiled young potatoes sprinkled with parsley, and buttered green peas and onions.

Makes 6 servings

2½ pounds veal
1 teaspoon freshly ground black pepper
2 tablespoons butter or margarine
Juice of 1 lemon
1 teaspoon salt
3 tablespoons dry bread crumbs
½ cup Chicken Broth, page 35, or bouillon

Cut veal into 6 equal pieces about ½ inch thick. Place each veal piece between plastic wrap. Using a meat mallet, pound veal until ¼ inch thick. Sprinkle both sides with pepper.

Melt butter in a large skillet over medium heat. Add veal; sauté until browned, 3 to 4 minutes on each side. Reduce heat to medium-low. Sprinkle lemon juice, salt, and bread crumbs on veal. Add broth to skillet. Cover and cook over medium-low heat until tender, 40 to 45 minutes, occasionally basting with cooking juices. Be careful not to wash bread crumbs from veal with baste. Serve hot.❧

Polish Beef

Wolowina po Polsku

Maggi seasoning is the Polish equivalent of soy sauce, available in most supermarkets.

Makes 6 servings

2½ to 3 pounds beef round steak, cut 1 inch thick
1¼ cups red wine
5 tablespoons vegetable oil
1 teaspoon Maggi seasoning
1 tablespoon salt
1 teaspoon freshly ground black pepper
2 tablespoons butter or margarine
2 medium onions, halved, sliced
1 pound fresh mushrooms, sliced
All-purpose flour
1 tablespoon cornstarch
2 tablespoons water

Cut beef into 5 × 3-inch oval pieces. Using a meat mallet, pound meat until about ½ inch thick. In a shallow 9- or 10-inch-square baking dish, combine wine, 2 tablespoons of the oil, Maggi seasoning, salt, and pepper. Place meat in wine mixture. Refrigerate for 1 hour, turning meat every 15 minutes.

Melt butter in a medium skillet over medium heat. Add onions; sauté until tender. Remove meat from marinade; place in a medium bowl. Pour marinade into a large skillet. Add mushrooms. Cook, uncovered, over medium heat until tender, 5 to 7 minutes. Add onions. Cook for 5 minutes over medium-low heat.

Place meat on a flat work surface. Evenly sprinkle flour on both sides of meat. Place on a rack. Let stand for 5 minutes.

Preheat oven to 350°F (175°C). Heat the remaining 3 tablespoons oil in a large skillet over medium-high heat. Add meat; sauté until browned. Arrange meat in a 9- or 10-inch-square baking dish. Spoon mushroom mixture over meat. Cover with foil or a tight-fitting lid.

Bake for 30 minutes, or until tender. Remove meat pieces to a warm platter and keep warm; reserve juices. In a small bowl, blend cornstarch and water; stir into cooking juices. Cook over medium heat until slightly thickened. Pour over meat. Serve hot.❧

Marinated Beef Roast

Marynowana Pieczen Wolowa

Leftovers of this roast make an excellent pierogi filling.

Makes 6 servings

Marinade

 2 cups dry red wine

 Juice from 1½ lemons

 ¼ cup water

 2 medium onions, quartered

 1 carrot, quartered

 1 parsley root, halved

 ½ celery root

 10 black peppercorns

 ¼ teaspoon ground thyme

 1 bay leaf

 1 (3-pound) lean boneless beef chuck roast

 Salt

 ½ teaspoon ground sweet paprika

 2 tablespoons vegetable oil

 ½ pint sour cream (1 cup)

 1 tablespoon all-purpose flour

Prepare Marinade: Combine all ingredients in a medium saucepan. Bring to a boil over medium heat. Boil for 1 to 2 minutes.

Place roast in a small, deep, nonmetallic baking dish. Add hot marinade, cool, then cover with plastic wrap or foil. Refrigerate for 2 days, turning roast twice each day.

Remove meat from marinade; reserve marinade. Pat roast dry with paper towels. Rub with salt. Sprinkle roast with paprika.

Preheat oven to 325°F (165°C). Heat oil in a medium skillet over medium-high heat. Add roast; brown on all sides. Transfer roast to a small, deep baking dish. Add reserved marinade. Cover and cook for 2 hours, basting with marinade every 15 minutes.

In a small bowl, combine sour cream and flour until smooth. Spoon sour cream mixture evenly over roast. Bake, uncovered, for 15 to 20 minutes, or until glaze forms and meat is tender. To serve, slice roast; place in a serving dish. Strain cooking juices; ladle over meat.

Beef Liver and Onions

Watrobka Wolowa z Cebulka

For a sweeter dish, try red onions.

Makes 4 to 6 servings

¼ cup all-purpose flour
1½ pounds sliced beef liver
¼ cup butter or margarine
4 medium onions, sliced, separated into rings
Salt
Freshly ground black pepper
1 cup dry red wine
1 tablespoon cornstarch (optional)
1 tablespoon water (optional)

Place flour in a shallow dish. Dip liver in flour until evenly coated.

Melt butter in a large skillet over medium-low heat. Add onions; sauté until tender. Transfer onions to a bowl. Add liver slices to skillet; sauté over medium heat until evenly browned, 4 to 5 minutes on each side. Season with salt and pepper to taste. Pour wine into skillet. Cover with a tight-fitting lid. Cook over medium-low heat until liver is tender, 8 to 10 minutes. Serve hot. If desired, thicken cooking juices with a mixture of cornstarch and water.❧

Hungarian Goulash

Wegierski Gulasz

Goulash is traditionally served over potatoes or noodles; it is also excellent with Potato Pancakes, page 76.

Makes 6 to 8 servings

1½ pounds lean beef, pork, or veal
2 tablespoons vegetable oil
2 medium onions, chopped
2 cups Beef Broth, page 34; Meat Broth, page 33; or bouillon
½ teaspoon ground sweet paprika
¼ teaspoon freshly ground black pepper
¼ teaspoon ground marjoram
2 medium green bell peppers, sliced into ½-inch strips
2 medium tomatoes, cut into wedges, or
1 tablespoon tomato paste
1 cup red wine
¼ cup water
1 tablespoon cornstarch
¼ teaspoon salt

Cut meat into ½- to ¾-inch cubes. Heat oil in a large skillet over medium-high heat. Add meat and onions; sauté until meat browns on all sides.

Place meat and onions in a medium saucepan. Add broth, paprika, black pepper, and marjoram. Cover and cook over medium heat for 50 minutes. Add bell peppers and tomatoes. Stir gently. Cover and cook for 10 minutes. Add wine. Cover and simmer over low heat for 10 minutes.

In a small cup, blend water and cornstarch until smooth. Stir into meat mixture. Season with salt. Bring to a boil; cook, stirring, until slightly thickened. Serve hot.❧

Roast Beef with Onion Stuffing

Pieczen Wolowa z Cebulowym Nadzieniem

I suggest sweet red onions for the stuffing.

Makes 8 servings

Onion Stuffing
  2 tablespoons butter or margarine
  2 medium onions, minced
  ¼ cup minced celery
  3 tablespoons dry bread crumbs

  1 tablespoon butter or margarine
  1 (4- to 4½-pound) rolled beef round or rump roast
  1 teaspoon salt
  2 medium onions, sliced ¼ inch thick
  ½ ounce dried mushrooms
  8 black peppercorns
  2 bay leaves
  1½ cups Meat Broth, page 33, or bouillon
  All-purpose flour

Prepare Onion Stuffing: In a medium skillet, melt butter over medium heat. Add onions, celery, and bread crumbs; sauté until onions are tender. Let cool.

Preheat oven to 325°F (165°C). Melt butter in a large skillet over medium-high heat. Add roast; sauté until browned on all sides, 5 to 7 minutes, turning. Place in a medium roasting pan. Pour cooking juices over roast. Sprinkle with salt. Impale whole onion slices on wooden picks, pressing slices against top and side of roast. Wash mushrooms. Arrange in pan around roast. Add peppercorns, bay leaves, and 1 cup of the broth. Cover and bake for 1½ hours, or until nearly tender. Baste roast with some of the remaining ½ cup broth every 15 to 20 minutes until all remaining broth is used. Remove from oven. Cool for 10 minutes.

Remove onion slices and wooden picks; discard. With a sharp knife, cut 6 to 8 deep pockets across the width of roast at 1- to 1¼-inch intervals, being careful not to cut through sides or bottom. Spoon Onion Stuffing into each pocket. Sprinkle a little flour over top of roast. Bake, uncovered, for 30 minutes, or until tender. Before serving, slice roast between pockets, so each serving contains stuffing. Serve hot on a platter, with pan juices. ❧

Ground-Beef Patties

Kotlety Wolowe

This dish is a favorite of Poles everywhere.

Makes 4 to 6 servings

1½ pounds lean ground beef
⅔ cup dry bread crumbs
¾ cup milk
1 egg, beaten
1 medium onion, minced
½ teaspoon ground sweet paprika
½ teaspoon salt
½ teaspoon freshly ground black pepper
¼ teaspoon garlic salt
3 tablespoons vegetable oil

In a large bowl, combine ground beef, ½ cup of the bread crumbs, milk, egg, onion, paprika, salt, pepper, and garlic salt. Shape beef mixture into patties. Lightly press both sides of each patty in remaining bread crumbs.

Heat oil in a large skillet over medium heat. Add patties; sauté until browned and cooked to desired doneness, 3 to 4 minutes on each side. Serve hot. ❧

Beef Ribs with Vegetables

Zeberka Wolowe z Warzywami

If necessary, add a little water or more broth to the roasting pan while cooking.

Makes 6 servings

3 tablespoons vegetable oil

1 clove garlic, minced

4½ to 5 pounds beef short ribs, cut in serving-size pieces

1 medium or large onion, sliced

7 medium carrots, peeled, halved, cut in 1½-inch pieces

1 teaspoon salt

½ teaspoon freshly ground black pepper

¼ teaspoon ground thyme

1½ cups Beef Broth, page 34, or bouillon

6 medium potatoes, peeled, quartered

1 (10-ounce) package frozen Brussels sprouts, partially thawed

Heat oil in a large skillet over medium-high heat. Add garlic; sauté for 2 minutes. Add ribs; sauté until ribs are browned on both sides, 8 minutes, turning once. Place ribs in a roasting pan.

Add onion and carrots to same skillet; sauté for 5 minutes, then add to roasting pan with ribs. Sprinkle salt, pepper, and thyme over ribs. Add broth and potatoes to roasting pan.

Cover and bake for 30 minutes, or until ribs and potatoes are almost tender. Add Brussels sprouts. Cook, uncovered, for 30 minutes, or until Brussels sprouts are heated throughout. Serve hot.

Meat Loaf with Eggs

Klops Nadziewany Jajami

This meat loaf is excellent served hot as a main dish, or cold as a sandwich filling.

Makes 10 to 12 servings

About 2 cups dry bread crumbs

¾ cup milk

2 tablespoons butter or margarine

2 medium onions, minced

2 pounds lean ground beef

1½ pounds lean ground pork

½ teaspoon garlic powder

1½ teaspoons salt

1 teaspoon freshly ground black pepper

2 eggs, beaten

¼ cup chopped fresh parsley

3 hard-cooked eggs, halved lengthwise

Preheat oven to 350°F (175°C). In a small bowl, soak 1½ cups of the bread crumbs in milk. Melt butter in a medium skillet over medium-high heat. Add onions; sauté until soft, 5 minutes.

In a large bowl, mix beef and pork. Add soaked bread crumbs, onions, garlic powder, salt, pepper, and beaten eggs; mix thoroughly.

On a large cutting board, sprinkle the remaining ½ cup bread crumbs evenly over a 13 × 12-inch rectangular area. Pat meat mixture over bread crumbs, using your hands or the flat side of a knife blade. Form meat into a 13 × 12-inch rectangle, about 1 inch thick. Sprinkle 2 tablespoons of the parsley over a 1-inch wide strip of meat mixture, about 3 inches in from a long side. Arrange halves of hard-cooked eggs, lengthwise, cut sides down, on top of parsley strip. Lightly press eggs into meat. Sprinkle remaining parsley over eggs. Roll meat, jelly-roll style, starting from long side closest to eggs, so eggs end up in center of meat loaf. When finished rolling, pat meat loaf ends until rounded.

Grease a deep 13 × 9-inch baking dish. Place meat loaf, seam side down, in pan. Bake, uncovered, for 1½ hours, or until done (170°F [75°C] on a meat thermometer). ❖

Bacon and Beef Rolls

Zrazjkj Wolowe

Beef rolls make a tasty party or picnic dish.

Makes 14 to 16 rolls

1 pound ground beef
¼ cup chopped dehydrated mushrooms or ½ cup chopped fresh mushrooms
1 egg
½ teaspoon salt
½ teaspoon ground marjoram
⅛ teaspoon freshly ground black pepper
⅛ teaspoon ground thyme
8 strips thin-sliced bacon, sliced lengthwise in half
1 cup Meat Broth, page 33, or beef bouillon
1 tablespoon cornstarch
½ cup cold water

In a medium bowl, combine beef, mushrooms, egg, salt, marjoram, pepper, and thyme. Form rolls about 1½ inches in diameter and 3 inches long. Wrap each roll tightly with a half strip of bacon. Place rolls in a large skillet so exposed ends of bacon are against bottom of pan. Brown rolls over medium heat until browned on all sides, about 15 to 20 minutes.

Preheat oven to 350°F (175°C). Arrange rolls in a shallow 9-inch-square baking dish. Add broth. Cover with a tight-fitting lid and bake for 1 hour. Remove rolls from juices. Pour juices into a small saucepan. Simmer over low heat.

In a small bowl, blend cornstarch and cold water until smooth. Stir into simmering sauce. Simmer, stirring, for 2 minutes. Serve hot over rolls. ⁂

Browned Beef

Befsztyk

An old standby Polish recipe, it was prepared when beef was available.

Makes 6 servings

2 pounds beef top round steak, ½ inch thick
½ cup plus 1 tablespoon all-purpose flour
¼ cup butter or margarine
2 medium onions, sliced
Salt
Freshly ground black pepper
1 cup Beef Broth, page 34, or bouillon

Slice beef into serving-size pieces. Place ½ cup flour in a shallow dish. Dip beef in flour until evenly coated.

Melt 2 tablespoons of the butter in a large skillet over medium heat. Add beef; sauté until both sides are browned. Remove beef from skillet; set aside.

Preheat oven to 325°F (165°C). Place onions in same skillet; sauté over medium heat until tender. Grease a 9- or 10-inch-square baking dish. Arrange onions in baking dish. Place beef on onions. Sprinkle with salt and pepper. Pour broth into baking dish. Cover with a tight-fitting lid. Bake for 1 hour, or until tender. Remove beef from baking dish; place on a hot platter. Strain and degrease cooking juices.

Melt the remaining 2 tablespoons butter in a small skillet. Add the 1 tablespoon flour; cook, stirring, over medium-low heat until golden brown. Stir in cooking juices. Cook over medium heat, stirring constantly, until thickened. Serve gravy over beef. ⁂

Beef Roll
Relay Wolowe

The broth used to prepare these versatile rolls can also be the main ingredient of a delicious gravy.

Makes 6 servings

2 (1- to 1½-pound) beef top round steaks
½ teaspoon salt
½ teaspoon freshly ground black pepper
½ cup milk
1 cup soft bread crumbs
3 eggs
2 hard-cooked eggs, coarsely chopped
1 pound lean ground beef
¼ cup chopped fresh parsley
¼ teaspoon dried marjoram
¼ teaspoon garlic powder
6 cups Beef Broth, page 34, or bouillon
3 tablespoons butter or margarine

Place each steak between plastic wrap. Using a meat mallet, pound each steak to about a 12 × 8-inch rectangle, ¼ to ⅜ inch thick. When pounding meat, do not use a straight up-and-down movement. Use a sliding action to stretch meat more than flatten. Sprinkle ⅛ teaspoon of the salt and ⅛ of the teaspoon pepper on inner side of each steak. Roll each steak tightly.

In a medium bowl, combine milk, bread crumbs, 2 of the raw eggs, hard-cooked eggs, ground beef, parsley, marjoram, garlic powder, and remaining salt and pepper. Unroll steak rectangles.

In a small bowl, beat the remaining 1 egg with a fork. Brush egg over inner side of each steak. Pat half of filling on each steak, making an even layer to within 1 inch from edges. Roll steaks tightly, lengthwise or widthwise, according to preference. Secure with wooden picks.

In a large pot, bring broth to a boil. Place each beef roll on a 20 × 16-inch piece of cheesecloth. Tightly roll each beef roll in cheesecloth. Tie ends closed with string. Wrap string several times along length of beef rolls. Place beef rolls in broth. Cook, covered, over medium-high heat for 1 hour. If broth does not cover beef rolls, turn rolls every 15 minutes. Remove from broth. Unwrap cheesecloth.

In a large skillet, melt butter over medium-high heat. Add beef rolls and brown, about 5 minutes. Slice and serve with cooking juices, if desired.

Variation
To serve cold, remove from broth. Let cool. When cool, cover and refrigerate overnight. Unwrap cheesecloth. Slice ⅜ inch thick. Serve as an appetizer or sandwich filling.

It's a good thing that the dessert chapter is last. Otherwise, the rest of this book might never have been written.

The list of Polish desserts, it seems, goes on forever—and with good reason: Polish pastries and desserts take a backseat to no others in the world. Indeed, if the Polish cook can be said to be deadly serious about anything, he or she is serious about desserts,

Here are cheesecakes, ice creams, and gelatin desserts. Also round jam-filled, powdered-sugar dusted doughnuts called *paczki* (PONCH-kee), creamy-frosted multilay-ered tortes; and mazurkas-frosted fruit and sugar-covered cookie crusts.

Within this chapter, you'll find cakes and rolls featuring poppy seeds and walnuts, spice cakes, and the photogenic Pyramid and Sculpture Cakes. You'll find airlike Cookie Crisps, which simply melt in your mouth.

Yes, the dessert chapter has the largest number of recipes in the book—and the shortest introduction. Short and sweet! Suffice it to say that occasions are thought up in Poland just so desserts can be served. Let the recipes speak for themselves! Onward, to desserts.

DESSERTS

Fruit Tarts

Owocowe Babeczki

Fruit tarts are traditionally made in small (about 4½-inch diameter) shallow baking pans in which the tart shell dough is formed and baked. If you don't have tart pans, you can use muffin or cupcake pans instead; just adjust the size of the rolled dough rounds to fit.

Makes 12 tarts

Tart Shells

    3 cups all-purpose flour

    ⅔ cup unsalted butter

    ¼ cup sugar

    2 egg yolks

    ¼ cup cold milk

Orange Glaze

    ½ cup sugar

    1 tablespoon cornstarch

    ½ cup orange juice

    ¼ cup water

    2 tablespoons lemon juice

    2 tablespoons orange liqueur

Almond Filling

    1½ cups dairy whipping cream

    ½ pound almond paste

    1 teaspoon vanilla extract

    1 tablespoon orange liqueur

    About 2 pints fresh blueberries, raspberries, or sliced strawberries

    Whipped cream to garnish (optional)

Prepare Tart Shells: In a food processor, combine flour, butter, and sugar into a mixture resembling coarse cornmeal. Place egg yolks and milk in a small bowl; beat lightly with a fork to combine. Add yolk mixture to flour mixture, process on and off for seconds at a time, until a rough dough forms. Remove dough from processor and gently shape dough into a ball. Cover and rest dough in a cool place or refrigerate for 30 minutes.

Preheat oven to 400°F (205°C). Divide dough into 12 equal pieces. Lightly butter 12 tart baking pans or an equal number of muffin or cupcake cups. For a 4½-inch tart pan, roll one piece dough into a 5½-inch round on a flat, smooth surface. Remove dough from board with a spatula. Using your fingertips, gently press dough round into bottom and sides of tart pan; make a shell resembling a miniature pie crust. Prick bottom of dough with a fork several times, so air bubbles will not form. Repeat with remaining 11 pieces of dough. Bake for 12 to 16 minutes, or until golden. Let shells cool in their baking pans.

Prepare Orange Glaze: Combine sugar and cornstarch in a small saucepan. Add orange juice, water, lemon juice, and orange liqueur. Bring to boil over medium-high heat, stirring with a metal whisk. Reduce heat to medium; cook until thickened to consistency of maple syrup. Remove from heat; let cool to room temperature. Makes 1 cup.

Prepare Almond Filling: Pour whipping cream into a large bowl; beat into a thick froth. Finely grate almond paste into whipped cream; add vanilla and orange liquor. Mix until combined. Makes 3 cups.

Rinse berries and pat dry. Spoon about 3 tablespoons of the filling into each Tart Shell. Arrange fruit on top. Trickle about 1½ tablespoons Orange Glaze over fruit on each tart; garnish with dollops of whipped cream (if using). Store in the refrigerator for up to 8 hours. Before serving, let stand at room temperature for 2 to 3 hours. ⁂

Sponge Cake
Biszkopt

Although regular all-purpose flour can be used, choosing any of the special cake flours such as Pillsbury SoftasSilk cake flour will result in a lighter, more delicate dessert.

Makes 1 (8-inch-round) 3-layer frosted sponge cake

Apricot Glaze
   1 cup apricot preserves
   2 tablespoons brandy

Chocolate-Almond Cream Filling
   2 (6-oz.) milk chocolate bars, broken into pieces
   ⅔ cup milk
   3 cups miniature marshmallows
   2 cups whipping cream
   2 tablespoons rum

Coffee Butter Cream Frosting
   4 egg yolks
   1 cup softened unsalted butter
   1½ cups sugar
   ¼ cup freshly made strong coffee
   1 tablespoon vanilla extract
   1 tablespoon Kahlúa or amaretto liquor

White Cake Batter
   6 eggs, separated
   1 cup sugar
   1 tablespoon vanilla, almond, or other extract
   1 tablespoon lemon juice
   Zest of 1 lemon, grated
   1½ cups cake flour
   1 teaspoon baking powder

Chocolate Cake Batter
   ½ cup cake flour
   ¼ teaspoon salt
   2 tablespoons unsweetened cocoa powder
   3 eggs, separated
   ½ cup sugar
   2 tablespoons lemon juice

   Chocolate shavings or slivered almonds to garnish (optional)

Prepare Apricot Glaze: Place apricot preserves in a blender; mix by turning blender on-off for a few seconds, 2 or 3 times. Do not puree. Place mixed preserves in a small saucepan. Bring to boil over medium heat. Add brandy. Stir to combine. Remove from heat; let cool. Makes about 1 cup.

Prepare Chocolate-Almond Cream Filling: Place a double boiler over medium-high heat. Melt chocolate in top of boiler. Stir milk into chocolate. Add marshmallows, stirring with a wire whisk until marshmallows melt. Remove from heat; let cool. In a large bowl, beat whipping cream until stiff; combine with chocolate mixture. Stir in rum; cover and refrigerate. Makes enough filling for an 8-inch, 3-layer cake.

Prepare Coffee Butter Cream Frosting: In a large bowl, beat egg yolks until thick and lemon colored; set aside. In large bowl of an electric mixer, beat butter until creamy. In a medium saucepan, combine sugar and coffee. Bring to boil over medium-high heat, stirring until sugar dissolves. Cook until sugar mixture reaches 236°F (115°C), or until temperature reaches soft-ball stage, where sugar-mixture balls form in cold water and can be flattened with fingertips. Pour hot sugar mixture into egg yolks, beating at high speed with electric mixer. Beat until mixture cools. Beat butter into egg yolk and sugar mixture, 1 tablespoon at a time, to make a smooth frosting. Beat in vanilla and liqueur. Cover and refrigerate for 30 min-

utes. Makes enough frosting for an 8-inch, 3-layer cake.

Prepare White Cake Batter: Place egg yolks and sugar in a large food processor bowl; process 2 to 3 minutes, until pale and creamy. Add vanilla, lemon juice, and lemon zest. Process 1 minute, or until combined. Sift flour and baking powder into a medium bowl. Add flour mixture to egg yolks and sugar. Process 2 minutes, or until blended into a smooth batter.

Place egg whites in a large bowl. Using an electric mixer on high speed, beat egg whites until stiff peaks form. Gently fold batter into beaten egg whites; combine into a smooth batter. Makes 2 (8-inch) cake layers.

Prepare Chocolate Cake Batter: Sift flour, salt, and cocoa into a medium bowl. Place egg yolks, sugar, and lemon juice in a large food processor bowl; process 2 minutes, or until creamy. Place egg whites in a large bowl. Using an electric mixer on high speed, beat egg whites until stiff peaks form.

Add flour mixture to egg yolk mixture; process 1 minute, until combined. Gently fold beaten egg whites into flour mixture, combining into a smooth batter. Makes 1 (8-inch) cake layer.

Preheat oven to 350°F (175°C). Using butter, grease sides and bottoms of 3 (8-inch round) cake pans. Cut 3 (8-inch round) pieces of waxed paper. Line bottoms of baking pans with waxed paper. Carefully pour equal amounts White Cake Batter into 2 pans. Pour Chocolate Cake Batter into third pan. Bake 20 to 25 minutes, or until a wooden pick inserted in center of cakes comes out clean. Turn cakes out of pans; let cool on racks.

If cake tops are uneven, use a long, sharp knife to carefully slice off just enough cake to make a level surface. Place one cooled white cake on a serving plate. Spread one-third of the Apricot Glaze on top. Carefully spread half of the Chocolate-Almond Cream Filling over the glaze. Top with chocolate-cake layer. Add another one-third of the glaze and the remaining filling on top of chocolate-cake layer. Place the other white cake on top, completing a 3-layered cake.

Top with remaining Apricot Glaze. Swirl Coffee Butter Cream Frosting on cake sides and over the Apricot Filling on top. Garnish with chocolate shavings or slivered almonds, if using. ❧

Apple Pancakes
Platcki z Jablkami

Make your own buttermilk for this recipe by mixing 1 teaspoon white vinegar with ½ cup milk and letting it stand at room temperature for about 10 minutes.

Makes about 14 pancakes

4 eggs, separated
¼ cup honey
6 tablespoons sugar
½ cup buttermilk
2 cups all-purpose flour
1 teaspoon baking powder
3 medium apples, peeled and cored
1 teaspoon fresh lemon juice
Light cream, if needed
Cinnamon sugar, maple syrup, whipped cream, confectioner's sugar, or any berry topping (optional)

In a food processor, combine egg yolks with honey, sugar, and buttermilk until smooth. In a large bowl, mix flour and baking powder; add to egg yolk mixture and process into a smooth batter. Transfer batter to a large bowl. With an electric mixer or in a clean food processor, beat egg whites until soft peaks form. Fold beaten egg whites into batter.

Grate apples into a medium bowl; add lemon juice and stir into apples to prevent browning. Mix grated apples into batter. If the batter is too stiff to pour, add up to ¼ cup cream to the batter.

Grease a large skillet or use a large skillet with a nonstick cooking surface; heat over medium-high heat. Using a ⅓-cup measuring cup for each pancake, pour pancake batter into heated skillet. Use a small spatula to scrape any batter that may otherwise stick inside the measuring cup. Cook pancakes for about 2 minutes, or until air bubbles form. Using a turner, carefully flip pancake and cook other side for 1 and 2 minutes, or until pancake is cooked through and lightly browned.

Serve plain or top with cinnamon sugar (if using).

Variation

For blueberry pancakes, substitute 2 cups whole fresh blueberries for apples and lemon juice. ❧

Strawberry Dessert

Krem Smietankowy z Truskawkami

A delightful dessert when strawberries are in their peak season.

Makes 4 to 6 servings

- 2 tablespoons unflavored gelatin powder
- 2 tablespoons cold water
- 1 tablespoon boiling water
- 1⅛ cups sweetened condensed milk
- ¼ cup sugar
- 2 tablespoons Vanilla Sugar, page 174
- 3 egg whites
- 1 pint fresh strawberries
- 2 ounces semisweet chocolate curls

Combine gelatin and cold water in a small bowl; let stand for 5 minutes to soften. Stir boiling water into gelatin mixture until dissolved. Refrigerate until slightly thickened.

In a large bowl, combine condensed milk, sugar, and Vanilla Sugar. Using an electric mixer, beat until thick and foamy, 5 minutes.

In a medium bowl, beat egg whites until stiff; fold into milk mixture. Fold thickened gelatin mixture into milk mixture. Pour into 4 to 6 dessert dishes. Refrigerate for 2 hours or until set. To serve, top with whole strawberries and chocolate curls.

Uncooked eggs should not be eaten by young children, the elderly, or anyone with a compromised immune system, because they may contain salmonella bacteria, which can cause serious illness.

Powdered egg whites or meringue powder is available and can be substituted for raw egg whites.

Grandmother's Sweet Bread
Babka

This dessert, a cross between cake and sweet bread, is often baked for Easter

Makes 2 (10-inch) cakes

Topping
   ¼ cup sugar
   ½ cup all-purpose flour
   1 teaspoon ground cinnamon
   ¼ cup unsalted butter or margarine, chilled

   3 (¼-ounce) packages active dry yeast
   (3 tablespoons)
   ¾ cup warm water (110°F, 45°C)
   1 tablespoon plus 1 cup sugar
   About 7¾ cups all-purpose flour
   1½ cups milk
   1¼ cups unsalted butter or margarine
   6 eggs
   2 egg yolks
   1½ teaspoons salt
   2 egg whites
   Powdered Sugar Icing, page 181 (optional)

Grease side and bottom of 2 (10-inch) tube pans.

Prepare Topping: In a small bowl, combine sugar, flour, and cinnamon. Using a pastry blender or 2 knives, cut in butter or margarine until mixture resembles coarse crumbs; set aside.

In a shallow, medium bowl, dissolve yeast in warm water. Add 1 tablespoon sugar and ½ cup of the flour; stir to combine. Cover; let stand in a warm place 5 to 10 minutes until foamy.

Heat milk and butter in a small saucepan until melted. Let stand until mixture cools to warm.

In a large bowl, beat eggs, egg yolks, and remaining 1 cup sugar until pale and frothy. Add cooled milk mixture, salt, and yeast mixture. Beat until smooth. Gradually beat in 4½ cups of the flour. Stir in enough remaining flour to make a soft dough. Turn out dough on a lightly floured surface. Knead dough into a soft, smooth dough. Divide dough in half. Arrange 1 part dough in each greased pan. Cover with a damp cloth; let rise in a warm place, free from drafts, until doubled in bulk, about 2 hours.

Preheat oven to 350°F (175°C). Lightly beat 2 egg whites in a small bowl until foamy. Brush egg whites on top of dough. Evenly sprinkle Topping over dough. Bake for 50 to 55 minutes, or until a wooden pick inserted in center comes out clean. Cool cakes in pans for 3 to 4 minutes on racks. Turn out of pans; cool completely on racks. Frost with Powdered Sugar Icing (if using).

Vanilla Sugar

Place 2 cups sugar and 2 vanilla beans in a small jar or container. Cover with airtight lid; set aside in a cool, dry place. Shake occasionally. Store for 2 weeks before using. Makes 2 cups.

Spice Cake
Piernik

A heavy spice cake, this is excellent with tea or coffee.

Makes 1 (9-inch-square) cake

3½ cups all-purpose flour
1 tablespoon baking powder
¼ teaspoon ground cloves
½ teaspoon ground cinnamon
½ teaspoon ground allspice
½ teaspoon salt
2 cups plus 3 tablespoons granulated sugar
1 cup plus 2 tablespoons warm water
2 eggs, separated
Powdered sugar

Preheat oven to 325°F (165°C). Grease a 9-inch-square baking pan. Sift together flour, baking powder, cloves, cinnamon, allspice, and salt; set aside.

In a medium saucepan, combine 2 cups granulated sugar and 1 cup warm water. Bring to a boil over medium heat, stirring occasionally. Reduce heat to medium-low; cook for 10 minutes, stirring constantly. Remove from heat.

In a small skillet, place 1 tablespoon of the sugar. Brown over medium-high heat, about 2 minutes, shaking pan occasionally. Watch carefully to avoid burning sugar. Add the 2 tablespoons water; remove from heat. Swirl water until combined with sugar.

Add browned sugar to sugar syrup in saucepan; stir to blend. Pour sugar mixture into a large bowl. In a small bowl, beat egg yolks and the remaining 2 tablespoons sugar vigorously with a fork, about 3 minutes. Stir into sugar mixture. Using an electric mixer, beat sugar mixture until smooth, 4 to 5 minutes. While beating, gradually add flour mixture.

In a medium bowl, beat egg whites until stiff peaks form; fold into batter. Pour batter into greased pan. Bake for 40 to 45 minutes, or until a wooden pick inserted in center comes out clean. Cool cake in pan for 2 to 3 minutes on a rack. Turn out of pan; cool completely on rack. Arrange a paper doily over cake. Sift powdered sugar over doily. Remove doily carefully. Do not cut cake until cool.

Variation
When cake cools, slice into 2 layers. Spread ¾ cup thick plum or cherry jam on top of bottom layer. Replace top cake layer. Sprinkle with powdered sugar. Or frost (optional).

Sand Cake
Babka Piaskowa

This delicious dessert is called sand cake because of its outer texture.

Makes 1 (10-inch) cake

6 eggs
1 cup granulated sugar
¾ cup plus 1 tablespoon butter or margarine, melted
1⅔ cups all-purpose flour
1 tablespoon baking powder
½ teaspoon salt
1 tablespoon Vanilla Sugar, page 174; rum extract; or 1 teaspoon vanilla extract
Sifted powdered sugar

Preheat oven to 350°F (175°C). Grease a 10-inch fluted pan or Bundt pan.

Using an electric mixer on high speed, beat eggs and granulated sugar until pale and creamy, at least 10 minutes. Blend in butter.

In a small bowl, combine flour, baking powder, salt, and Vanilla Sugar. Fold dry ingredients into egg mixture until smooth. If using rum or vanilla extract, stir directly into egg mixture. Pour batter into greased pan.

Bake for 40 to 45 minutes, or until a wooden pick inserted in center comes out clean. Cool cake in pan for 2 to 3 minutes on a rack. Turn out of pan; cool completely on rack. Sprinkle with powdered sugar. ❧

Fancy Fruitcake
Keks

Give these delicious loaves to close friends and relatives for Christmas.

Makes 2 fruitcakes

¼ cup dry bread crumbs
1½ cups unsalted butter or margarine, at room temperature
1 cup sugar
5 eggs
2 tablespoons Polish vodka or other vodka
1 tablespoon vanilla extract
1⅞ cups instant flour, such as Wondra quick-mixing flour
2 tablespoons baking powder
¾ cup candied orange peel
½ cup chopped walnuts
¾ cup seedless raisins
½ cup chopped pitted prunes

Preheat oven to 350°F (175°C). Line 2 (8 × 4-inch) bread pans with foil so ends overlap pan sides; grease foil. Sprinkle bread crumbs evenly over greased foil.

In a large bowl, beat butter and sugar until smooth and creamy, 5 minutes. Add eggs, 1 at a time, beating after each addition until smooth. Blend in vodka and vanilla. Reserve 3 tablespoons flour. Gradually add remaining flour and baking powder to mixture, stirring until smooth.

In a small bowl, combine orange peel, walnuts, raisins, prunes, and reserved flour; toss to coat nuts and fruit. Work fruit and nut mixture into dough.

Divide dough between prepared pans. Bake for 35 to 40 minutes, or until a wooden pick inserted in center comes out clean. Remove loaves from pans by lifting foil. Cool completely on a rack. ❧

Sculpture Cake
Kolacz Weselny

This very old recipe is famous for the artistic, decorative sculpture arranged on top.

Makes 1 (10-inch) cake

Cheese Filling
    2 pounds dry cottage cheese or farmer's
    old-fashioned white cheese (4 cups)
    4 egg yolks
    2 cups sugar
    1 tablespoon Vanilla Sugar, page 174

    2 (¼-ounce) packages active dry yeast
    (2 tablespoons)
    1 cup plus 1 tablespoon sugar
    ¼ cup warm water
    1 cup unsalted butter or margarine, at room
    temperature
    2 eggs
    1 pint warm milk (2 cups), plus milk for
    brushing dough
    6½ cups all-purpose flour
    Pinch salt

Prepare Cheese Filling: With a grinder or food processor fitted with a metal blade, process cheese. Do not puree or overprocess. Place egg yolks, sugar, and Vanilla Sugar in a large bowl. Beat until pale and creamy, at least 10 minutes. Add cheese, a little at a time, while beating. Beat until smooth; set aside.

In a small bowl, dissolve yeast and the 1 tablespoon sugar in warm water. Let stand until foamy, 5 to 10 minutes. Place the 1 cup sugar, butter, and eggs in a large bowl. Beat until pale and fluffy. Add yeast mixture, milk, 2 cups of the flour, and salt. Beat until well blended. Stir in enough remaining flour to make a soft dough. Turn out dough on a lightly floured surface. Clean and grease bowl. Knead dough until smooth and elastic. Place dough in greased bowl, turning to coat all sides. Cover with a clean damp cloth; let rise in a warm place, free from drafts, until doubled in bulk.

Preheat oven to 350°F (175°C). Grease side and bottom of a 10-inch springform pan. Divide dough into thirds. Using your hands, gently press one-third of dough evenly over bottom and side of pan. Evenly spread Cheese Filling over dough-lined pan. On a lightly floured surface, roll out another one-third of dough to a 10-inch circle. Place over Cheese Filling. Gently pat with your hands. Using a pastry brush, lightly brush milk over top of dough. Cut remaining one-third of dough in 4 even pieces. Shape 3 pieces into long ropes. Braid ropes; apply to outer edge of cake. Using remaining dough, cut desired figures with various cutters or form shapes with your hands. Arrange figures on top of dough as desired. Lightly brush with milk. Bake for 50 to 60 minutes, or until golden brown. Cool cake in pan for 5 minutes on a rack. Remove pan side; cool completely on rack.

Cream Cake
Garbusia

Make sure you use regular—not instant—vanilla pudding mix in this sweet favorite.

Makes 1 (9- or 10-inch) cake

Cream Mixture
   1 (3- to 3½-ounce) package vanilla pudding mix
   1 cup powdered sugar
   2 tablespoons all-purpose flour
   2½ cups whole milk
   1 cup butter or margarine, at room temperature
   2 tablespoons orange liqueur

Cake Batter
   1 cup water
   ½ cup butter or margarine
   1 cup all-purpose flour
   5 eggs
   1 teaspoon baking powder

Chocolate Glaze
   2 tablespoons butter or margarine
   2 tablespoons whole milk
   2 tablespoons unsweetened cocoa powder
   ½ cup powdered sugar

Prepare Cream Mixture: In a medium saucepan, combine pudding mix, sugar, and flour. Add milk. Bring to a boil over medium-high heat, stirring constantly. Boil 2 minutes, stirring until mixture becomes smooth and glossy. Let cool. In a large bowl, beat butter with an electric mixer. Slowly add pudding while mixing. Add orange liqueur and mix until smooth, 1 minute. Cover and refrigerate until needed.

Prepare Cake Batter: In a large saucepan, bring water and butter to a boil over medium heat. Slowly add flour, stirring constantly with a wooden spoon. When flour mixture becomes smooth and glossy, remove from heat. Add 1 egg and stir until smooth. Repeat with remaining eggs, one at a time. Add baking powder. Beat until batter is smooth.

Preheat oven to 400°F (205°C). Grease 3 shallow 9- or 10-inch round cake pans. Pour one-third of cake batter into each pan. Bake for 25 to 30 minutes, or until golden. Turn cakes out from pans and let cool. Place one cake on a large serving platter. Spoon half of the cream mixture over top of cake on platter. Place second cake on top of first cake. Spread with remaining cream mixture. Top with third cake.

Prepare Chocolate Glaze: In a small saucepan, melt butter over medium-high heat. Add remaining ingredients, stirring constantly. Bring mixture to a boil. Remove from heat. Cool slightly but use while glaze is warm enough to pour easily.

Frost top of cake with Chocolate Glaze, spreading chocolate so it drips down the cake sides. Cut into serving pieces.

Variation
Instead of orange liqueur, add 1 teaspoon instant coffee dissolved in 1 teaspoon hot water, or add 1 tablespoon coffee-flavored liqueur, rum, or peach-flavored schnapps. ❧

Chocolate Cake

Babka Czekoladowa

This is the Polish version of one of the most popular cakes in the world.

Makes 1 (9-inch) cake

5 eggs
1 cup sugar
1 cup plus 2 tablespoons butter or margarine, melted
5 ounces semisweet chocolate, melted
Juice of ½ lemon
Freshly grated peel of 1 lemon
1½ cups cake flour
1 teaspoon baking powder
½ teaspoon baking soda
½ teaspoon salt
Chocolate Frosting
2 teaspoons butter or margarine
3 ounces semisweet chocolate
1 tablespoon water
1 teaspoon lemon juice
1 teaspoon vanilla extract
About 1 cup sifted powdered sugar

Preheat oven to 350°F (175°C). Grease and flour a 9-inch tube pan.

In a large bowl, beat eggs and sugar until pale and creamy. Add butter, chocolate, lemon juice, and lemon peel. Beat until smooth, at least 5 minutes.

In a small bowl, sift together cake flour, baking powder, baking soda, and salt. Gradually add dry ingredients to egg mixture, beating constantly. Beat until smooth. Pour batter into prepared pan. Bake for 45 minutes or until a wooden pick inserted in center comes out clean. Cool cake in pan for 2 to 3 minutes on a rack. Turn out of pan; cool completely on rack.

Prepare Chocolate Frosting: Melt butter and chocolate in a small saucepan over low heat. Remove from heat. Stir in water, lemon juice, and vanilla. Stir about 1 cup powdered sugar into chocolate mixture. If frosting is too thin, add more sifted powdered sugar. If too thick, add a little hot water.

Drizzle or spread warm frosting over cooled cake. Let stand at room temperature until frosting sets.

Powdered Sugar Icing

Lukier

The thin, satin-smooth crust of this icing is a nice complement to cookies, mazurkas, and cakes.

Makes about 1¼ cups icing

2 egg whites
1½ cups sifted powdered sugar
½ teaspoon lemon juice

In a medium bowl, beat egg whites until frothy. Gradually add powdered sugar, beating constantly. Beat until glossy, 10 minutes. Add lemon juice; beat until icing stands up in soft peaks, 2 minutes.

Variation
Add food coloring or flavorings, such as 1 teaspoon sifted unsweetened cocoa powder or vanilla extract. Use a little more sugar if liquids are added.

Note
Uncooked eggs should not be eaten by young children, the elderly, or anyone with a compromised immune system, because they may contain salmonella bacteria, which can cause serious illness.

Powdered egg whites or meringue powder is available and can be substituted for raw egg whites.

Pyramid Cake

Sekacz

Both the consistency and flavor of this attractive cake improve with age.

Makes 1 (10-inch) cake

3 tablespoons dry bread crumbs
1 cup plus 1 tablespoon unsalted butter or margarine, at room temperature
1⅛ cups sugar
7 eggs, separated
1 tablespoon vanilla extract
2 tablespoons rum
1⅛ cups instant flour, such as Wondra quick-mixing flour
2 teaspoons baking powder
¾ cup potato starch or cornstarch

Grease a 10-inch tube pan. Evenly sprinkle bread crumbs over bottom.

In a large bowl, beat butter and sugar until light and fluffy, about 5 minutes. Add egg yolks, 1 at a time, beating until smooth after each addition. Beat until pale and fluffy. Add vanilla and rum.

Preheat a broiler. Adjust oven rack so top rim of pan is 6 inches from broiler. In a medium bowl, combine flour, baking powder, and potato starch; fold into egg mixture. Divide resulting mixture into 2 equal parts in 2 medium bowls. Divide egg whites into 2 equal portions; place in 2 other medium bowls. Beat 1 part egg white until stiff but not dry. Fold into 1 part flour mixture, until smooth. Pour ⅓ cup egg white and flour batter on bottom of prepared pan. Broil for 1 to 2 minutes, or until golden brown. Remove from oven.

Pour another ⅓ cup batter on top of first layer. Return to oven; broil for 1 to 2 minutes. Add layers until first portion of batter is used. Prepare second portion of batter by beating remaining egg whites until stiff peaks form; fold into flour mixture. Keep adding and baking thin layers of batter, ⅓ cup at a time, until all batter is used. Insert a wooden pick in center of cake. If pick does not come out clean, broil until pick is clean. Turn cake out of pan; cool on a rack.❖

Baked Cheesecake
Sernik

Chopped walnuts lend a delicious flavor and crispy texture to the crust of this favorite dessert.

Makes 1 (13 × 9-inch) cheesecake

Crust
⅓ cup granulated sugar
¼ cup packed light brown sugar
¼ cup unsalted butter or margarine, at room temperature
¾ cup all-purpose flour
¼ teaspoon baking powder
⅛ teaspoon salt
½ cup finely chopped walnuts

3 (8-ounce) packages cream cheese, at room temperature
1½ cups sugar
6 eggs, separated
¼ cup lemon juice
1 tablespoon rum extract
6 tablespoons all-purpose flour
½ pint whipping cream (1 cup)

Prepare Crust: Preheat oven to 350°F (175°C). Grease a (13 × 9-inch) baking pan. In a large bowl, cream together granulated sugar, brown sugar, and butter. Blend in flour, baking powder, salt, and walnuts to form a stiff dough. Press dough evenly over bottom of greased pan. Bake for 12 minutes, or until golden. Let cool.

Preheat oven to 325°F (165°C). In a large bowl, beat cream cheese until soft and creamy, 10 minutes. Add sugar; beat for 3 minutes. Add egg yolks, 1 at a time, beating constantly. Add lemon juice, rum extract, and flour; beat until smooth.

In a large bowl, beat egg whites until stiff peaks form. Fold egg whites into cheese mixture. Beat whipping cream in a medium bowl; fold into cheese mixture. Pour cheese mixture over baked crust. Bake for 1 hour, or until a wooden pick inserted in center comes out clean. Turn off oven; let cheesecake stand in oven for 1 hour. Remove from oven; cool, then cover and refrigerate for 12 hours before serving. ❧

Strawberry Gelatin
Pianka Truskawkowa

Here's a strawberry recipe that can be prepared year-round.

Makes 4 servings

½ pound frozen whole strawberries
1 tablespoon powdered sugar
1 tablespoon unflavored gelatin powder
3 tablespoons cold water
3 egg whites
3 tablespoons granulated sugar
Sliced strawberries or thin lemon slices (optional)

Place frozen strawberries in a medium bowl; sprinkle with powdered sugar. Let stand for 30 minutes or until thawed. Drain strawberry juice into a small saucepan.

Blend gelatin and cold water in a small bowl; let stand until gelatin is softened, 5 minutes. Bring strawberry juice to a boil over medium heat. Stir gelatin mixture into boiling strawberry juice. Refrigerate until slightly thick.

In a medium bowl, beat egg whites until soft peaks form. Gradually add granulated sugar, beating constantly until stiff peaks form. Carefully fold strawberries into egg-white mixture. Fold gelatin mixture into egg-white mixture.

Refrigerate until set. Serve chilled, decorated with several sliced strawberries (if using).

Note

Uncooked eggs should not be eaten by young children, the elderly, or anyone with a compromised immune system, because they may contain salmonella bacteria, which can cause serious illness.

Powdered egg whites or meringue powder is available and can be substituted for raw egg whites.❧

Plum Cake

Placek ze Sliwkami

Make sure you use only fresh ripe plums for this aromatic and attractive dessert.

Makes 1 (10-inch) cake

2 cups all-purpose flour

½ cup plus 3 tablespoons butter or margarine, at room temperature

3 tablespoons sour cream

½ cup powdered sugar

1 egg yolk

1 teaspoon vanilla extract

Freshly grated peel of 1 lemon

1½ pounds fresh plums

3 tablespoons powdered sugar, sifted

1½ teaspoons Vanilla Sugar, page 174

Place flour in a large bowl. Add butter, sour cream, ½ cup powdered sugar, egg yolk, vanilla extract, and lemon peel. Work flour mixture with your hands into a medium-soft dough. Press dough into a ball. Cover and refrigerate for 30 minutes.

Preheat oven to 430°F (220°C). Slice dough into round pieces approximately ½ inch thick. Butter sides and bottom of a round 10-inch springform baking pan. Reserve 1 dough-end slice, then place remaining dough slices in a flat layer on pan bottom. Press dough slices together and smooth dough with your fingertips. Roll reserved dough piece into a rope about ¼ inch thick. Place dough rope along inside, against bottom dough layer. Gently press rope into bottom dough and edge of pan sides.

Halve plums lengthwise and remove pits. Arrange plums, cut sides up, on bottom dough layer. Gently press plums into dough.

Bake for 20 to 25 minutes, or until a wooden pick inserted in center of cake comes out clean. Remove from oven. Combine the 3 tablespoons powdered sugar and Vanilla Sugar in a small bowl. Sprinkle sugar mixture over plums. Let cool.❧

Crispy-Crust Cheesecake

Sernik

Of all the Polish cheesecakes, this is one of my favorites.

Makes 1 (10-inch) cake

Cheesecake Crust

    1⅔ cups all-purpose flour

    ½ cup plus 1 tablespoon unsalted butter or margarine, chilled

    ⅓ cup sugar

    1 teaspoon baking powder

    1 tablespoon sifted unsweetened cocoa powder

    1 tablespoon sour cream

    8 eggs, separated

    ⅔ cup sugar

    1¾ to 2 cups dry cottage cheese

    2 tablespoons unsalted butter or margarine, at room temperature

    2 (8-ounce) packages cream cheese, at room temperature

    1 tablespoon vanilla extract

    1 (3- to 3½-ounce) package vanilla pudding mix

    Juice of 1 lemon

Prepare Cheesecake Crust: Sift flour into a medium bowl. Using a pastry blender or 2 knives, cut butter into small pieces; add to flour. Work butter into flour until mixture resembles coarse crumbs. Add sugar, baking powder, cocoa, and sour cream; knead into a smooth dough. Divide dough into 2 equal portions. Wrap both portions in plastic wrap or foil. Place in freezer for 30 minutes.

Preheat oven to 375°F (190°C). Grease bottom and side of a 10-inch springform pan. Remove 1 portion dough from freezer. Using a hand shredder, roughly shred 1 portion of frozen dough evenly onto bottom of pan. Bake for 4 to 5 minutes, or until golden brown. Cool.

Reduce oven temperature to 350°F (175°C). In a large bowl, beat egg yolks and sugar until pale and creamy. With a hand grinder, grind cottage cheese into a large bowl. Add cottage cheese, butter, cream cheese, vanilla, pudding mix, and lemon juice to egg-yolk mixture. Beat until smooth, 8 to 10 minutes.

In a medium bowl, beat egg whites until stiff but not dry; fold into cheese mixture. Spoon cheese filling onto baked crust; smooth surface. Shred remaining portion of frozen dough evenly over cheese filling. Bake for 1½ hours, or until a wooden pick inserted in center comes out clean. Cool on a rack for at least 2 hours before serving. ❧

Fruit Smoothies

Napoj Owocowy

A nutritious Polish milkshake.

Makes 4 to 6 servings

1 pound fresh or frozen strawberries,
blueberries, or pitted cherries
4 egg yolks (see note below)
3 tablespoons powdered sugar
1 pint milk (2 cups)
Ice cubes
1 teaspoon grated orange peel or lemon peel

Place fruit in a blender or food processor fitted with a metal blade; process until pureed. Place egg yolks and sugar in a large bowl; beat until fluffy. Add milk, beating until smooth. Add fruit; beat until smooth. Place 2 ice cubes in each of 4 to 6 serving glasses. Pour fruit drink into glasses. Garnish with orange peel. Serve immediately.

Note
Uncooked eggs should not be eaten by young children, the elderly, or anyone with a compromised immune system, because they may contain salmonella bacteria, which can cause serious illness.

Pasteurized eggs are available in some markets and can be safely used in uncooked dishes.⁕

Poppy Seed Rolls

Strucle z Makiem

Poppy Seed Rolls are a classic Polish dessert.

Makes 2 rolls, approximately 17 to 19 inches long

Poppy Seed Filling
1 pound poppy seeds
1 cup granulated sugar
1 tablespoon Vanilla Sugar, page 174
2 tablespoons butter or margarine
1 egg, slightly beaten
¼ cup honey
¼ cup candied orange peel
¼ cup candied lemon peel
½ cup chopped walnuts
½ cup golden raisins
2 egg whites

Dough
2 (¼-ounce) packages active dry yeast
(2 tablespoons)
¼ cup warm water (110°F, 45°C)
1 tablespoon granulated sugar
4½ to 5½ cups all-purpose flour
¾ cup butter or margarine, chilled
3 eggs
3 egg yolks
½ cup sour cream
1 cup powdered sugar
1 tablespoon vanilla extract
½ teaspoon salt
Grated peel from 1 lemon

Prepare Poppy Seed Filling: Place poppy seeds in a medium saucepan. Cover with 2 to 3 cups water. Bring to a boil over medium heat. Remove from heat and let stand until cool. Rinse poppy seeds until water is clear, not milky. Carefully strain poppy seeds through a fine-mesh strainer; discard liquid. Stir granulated sugar and Vanilla Sugar into poppy seeds.

Using a hand grinder, grind poppy seeds into a medium bowl. Grind seeds two more times. Melt butter in a large skillet. Add poppy seed mixture. Simmer over low heat for 15 to 20 minutes, stirring occasionally. Stir in egg, honey, orange peel, lemon peel, walnuts, and raisins. In a medium bowl, beat egg whites until stiff peaks form; fold into poppy seed mixture. Cool mixture.

To make the dough: Grease 2 baking sheets. In a small bowl, dissolve yeast in warm water. Stir in granulated sugar and 2 tablespoons of the flour. Let stand until foamy, 5 to 10 minutes.

Sift 4 cups flour into a large bowl. Cut butter into small pieces; add to flour. Using a pastry blender or 2 knives, cut in butter until mixture resembles coarse crumbs. Add 2 of the eggs, egg yolks, sour cream, powdered sugar, vanilla, salt, lemon peel, and yeast mixture. Work with your hands or heavy-duty electric mixer into a soft dough.

Turn out dough on a lightly floured surface. Knead dough until smooth and elastic, 8 to 10 minutes. Divide dough into 2 equal parts. On a lightly floured surface, roll each part into a 15- to 16-inch square. Spread Poppy Seed Filling evenly 2 inches in from all sides of dough. Roll up dough squares, jelly-roll style. Pinch ends to seal. Place seam side down on greased baking sheets. Cover and let rise in a warm place, free from drafts, until doubled in bulk.

Preheat oven to 350°F (175°C). Bake for 35 minutes. Remove from oven. Lightly beat remaining egg and brush over rolls. Bake for 5 to 10 minutes longer, or until golden brown. Cool rolls on a rack. To serve, slice in 1- or 1½-inch pieces.

Variations
Substitute 2 (12½-ounce) cans poppy seed filling for poppy seeds, sugar, and Vanilla Sugar. Combine with remaining filling ingredients as directed.

Honey may be omitted for a less sweet filling.

Nut Roll

Rolada Orzechowa

One batch makes several rolls, great for entertaining large groups.

Makes 8 (14- to 16-inch) nut rolls

4 (¼-ounce) packages active dry yeast
(4 tablespoons)

½ cup warm water (110°F, 45°C)

½ cup granulated sugar

1 (12-ounce) can evaporated milk, warmed

7¾ cups all-purpose flour

3 eggs

2 cups butter or margarine, melted, cooled

1 teaspoon salt

1 teaspoon vanilla extract

4 pounds walnuts, finely chopped

1½ cups powdered sugar

½ cup honey

1 egg blended with 1 tablespoon granulated
sugar for glaze (see note on page 186
concerning uncooked eggs)

In a medium bowl, dissolve yeast in warm water. Stir in ¼ cup of the granulated sugar, milk, and ¼ cup of the flour. Let stand until foamy, 5 to 10 minutes.

In a medium bowl, beat eggs and the remaining ¼ cup granulated sugar until pale and creamy. Stir in butter, salt, and vanilla. Stir egg mixture into yeast mixture along with 1 cup flour. Stir in enough flour to make a soft dough.

Turn out dough onto a lightly floured surface. Clean and grease bowl. Knead dough until smooth and elastic, 8 to 10 minutes, adding flour as needed. Place dough in greased bowl. Cover and refrigerate 3 hours or overnight.

In a medium bowl, combine walnuts, powdered sugar, and ¾ cup of the remaining flour. Divide refrigerated dough into 8 equal portions. Cover and refrigerate 7 parts until needed.

Preheat oven to 350°F (175°C). Grease 2 to 3 large baking sheets. On a lightly floured surface, roll out 1 part dough into an about 14 × 8-inch oval. Evenly spread a generous 1 cup of the walnut mixture over rolled dough. Drizzle 1 tablespoon honey over walnut mixture. Working quickly so dough does not get warm, roll up dough lengthwise, jelly-roll style. Place nut roll, seam-side down, on greased baking sheet. Repeat with remaining dough, walnut mixture, and honey, arranging nut rolls on greased baking sheets. Allow room for spreading during baking.

Bake for 15 to 20 minutes, or until golden brown. Brush tops of nut rolls with egg glaze immediately upon removal from oven. Cool on a rack. To serve, slice into 1-inch pieces; arrange on a platter. (Rolls can be tightly wrapped and frozen for up to 3 months.) ❧

Meringue Crisps

Bezy

Store these airy sweets in airtight containers to keep them crisp.

Makes about 50 cookies

2 egg whites
⅔ cup sifted powdered sugar
1 teaspoon vanilla extract
1 teaspoon lemon juice
1 tablespoon sifted unsweetened cocoa powder (optional)
¼ cup finely chopped walnuts (optional)

Preheat oven to 200°F (95°C). Grease a baking sheet.

Place egg whites in top of a double boiler; beat until stiff. Gradually add powdered sugar, beating constantly. Place double boiler over 1 inch of boiling water. Beat over low heat until smooth and glossy, 8 to 10 minutes. Add vanilla and lemon juice. Add cocoa and walnuts (if using). Beat for 1 minute to blend.

Place heaping teaspoons of mixture on greased baking sheet. Or, using a pastry bag fitted with a fluted nozzle, pipe by heaping teaspoons onto baking sheet. Bake for about 1¼ hours, or until hard and crisp; turn oven off and let cool in oven.

Filled Doughnuts

Paczki

Use your imagination and try any cream or fruit filling that meets your fancy.

Makes 50 to 60 doughnuts

4 (¼-ounce) packages active dry yeast (4 tablespoons)
⅓ cup warm water (110°F, 45°C)
2 tablespoons plus 1 cup granulated sugar
6¾ cups all-purpose flour
1¼ cups milk, warmed (110°F, 45°C)
12 egg yolks
1 teaspoon salt
½ teaspoon vanilla extract
½ cup butter, melted, cooled
½ cup margarine, melted, cooled
2 tablespoons Polish spiritus or rum
About ¾ cup thick cherry jam or other favorite jam
Vegetable oil
Powdered sugar

Grease 3 baking sheets. In a medium bowl, dissolve yeast in water. Stir in the 2 tablespoons granulated sugar and ¼ cup of the flour. Blend in milk until smooth. Let stand until foamy, 5 to 10 minutes.

In a large bowl, beat egg yolks, 1 cup granulated sugar, salt, and vanilla until pale and creamy. Add yeast mixture, butter, margarine,

3 cups of the flour, and spiritus. Work mixture into a soft dough, adding flour as needed. Turn out dough on a lightly floured surface. Clean and grease bowl. Knead dough until smooth and elastic, 8 to 10 minutes, working in additional flour as needed. Place dough in greased bowl, turning to coat all sides. Cover and let rise in a warm place, free from drafts, until doubled in bulk, about 2 to 2½ hours.

On a flat surface, roll out about 1 cup dough until ¼ inch thick. Keep remaining dough covered to prevent drying. Using a 2½-inch round cutter, cut out dough. Place ½ teaspoon cherry jam on 1 dough round. Lightly place another dough round directly on top of the first, covering jam. Using your fingers, crimp dough edges together tightly to prevent halves from separating during frying. Place filled doughnut on a flat work surface. Using a 2¼-inch round cutter, press over doughnut so crimped rough edge gets trimmed smooth and round. Place filled doughnut on a lightly greased baking sheet. Repeat process with remaining dough and jam until all baking sheets are filled, being careful to leave enough room between each doughnut for spreading when dough rises. Cover each baking sheet of doughnuts with a clean cloth. Let rise in a warm place, free from drafts, until doubled in bulk, about 1 hour.

Pour oil in a deep fryer or large saucepan to a depth of about 5 inches. Heat to 360°F (180°C), or until a 1-inch bread cube turns golden brown in 60 seconds. Add doughnuts without crowding, raised or top side down, so bottom will round out during cooking. Fry until golden brown, 3 to 4 minutes. Turn and fry other side until golden brown on both sides, about 3 minutes. Drain on paper towels. Dust doughnuts with powdered sugar. ❧

Hot Apple Drink
Kompot z Jablek

Enjoy this steaming hot beverage after a chilly fall hayride or winter skiing party.

Makes 6 to 8 servings

> 2 pounds firm tart apples, peeled
> 6 cups water
> About 6 tablespoons sugar
> 6 to 8 (3-inch) cinnamon sticks

Cut each apple into 8 pieces. Place apple pieces and water in a large saucepan; bring to a boil. Reduce heat and simmer, covered, over medium-low heat for 15 minutes. Add sugar to taste. Ladle hot liquid and apple pieces into serving cups or glasses. Add a cinnamon stick to each cup. ❧

Snowdrop Cherries

Wisnie Sniezyczka

For variety, try this recipe using half sweet and half sour cherries.

Makes 6 to 8 dessert servings

¾ cup granulated sugar

2 egg whites

1 tablespoon Vanilla Sugar, page 174

About 1¼ pounds fresh whole sweet or sour cherries with stems

Preheat oven to 250°F (120°C). Line a baking sheet with foil. Evenly sprinkle ¼ cup of the sugar over foil. Place egg whites in a small bowl and beat lightly with a fork.

In a small bowl, combine the remaining ½ cup sugar with Vanilla Sugar. Dip 1 cherry in egg whites. Let excess drip off, then roll cherry in sugar mixture in bowl until sugar evenly coats cherry. Place on sugared foil. Repeat process with remaining cherries. Bake for 20 minutes. Let cool. Serve chilled.

Orange-Lemon Mazurka

Pomaranczowo-Cytrynowy Mazurek

Aging the crust results in a texture that melts in your mouth.

Makes about 16 servings

2 cups all-purpose flour

1 cup unsalted butter or margarine, chilled

2 egg yolks

¾ cup powdered sugar

Freshly grated peel of 2 medium oranges

Freshly grated peel of 1 lemon

2 large tart apples, peeled, shredded

1¼ cups granulated sugar

½ cup slivered almonds

Sift flour into a medium bowl. Cut butter into small pieces; work into flour until mixture resembles coarse crumbs. Add egg yolks and powdered sugar; work quickly into a rough dough. Press dough into a ball. Wrap and refrigerate for 2 hours.

Preheat oven to 450°F (230°C). Grease a 9-inch-square baking pan. On a lightly floured surface, roll dough to a 10-inch square. Using a sharp knife, trim off 1-inch dough from each side; reserve dough scraps. Lightly flour rolled dough; roll onto a rolling pin. Unroll dough into greased pan. Roll remaining dough scraps into a ¼-inch rope, Arrange dough rope around pan edges on bottom layer of dough, lightly pressing rope into dough. Gently crimp top of dough rope along pan sides, like pie crust.

Bake for 15 to 20 minutes, or until golden brown; cool. Cover and refrigerate 5 or 6 days. Combine orange and lemon peel, apples, and granulated sugar in a medium saucepan. Simmer, uncovered, over low heat until thick, 20 to 25 minutes, stirring occasionally. Spoon hot filling over crust. Decorate with slivered almonds; cool. To serve, cut into squares.❧

Honey-Walnut Mazurka

Miodowo-Orzechowy Mazurek

I prepare this rich dessert for friends during the Christmas holidays.

Makes 20 to 24 servings

2½ cups all-purpose flour

2½ cups instant flour, such as Wondra quick-mixing flour

2 teaspoons baking powder

1 cup unsalted butter or margarine, chilled

1 cup granulated sugar

4 egg yolks

½ pint sour cream (1 cup)

1 tablespoon vanilla extract

3 cups finely chopped walnuts

⅓ cup powdered sugar

2 cups apricot preserves

¼ cup honey

In a large bowl, combine all-purpose flour, instant flour, and baking powder. Cut butter into small pieces; add to flour mixture. Work butter into flour until mixture resembles coarse crumbs. Add granulated sugar, egg yolks, sour cream, and vanilla; knead into a smooth dough. Cover with foil or plastic wrap; refrigerate overnight.

In a medium bowl, combine walnuts and powdered sugar. Preheat oven to 350°F (175°C). Divide dough into 3 equal parts. On a lightly floured surface, roll 1 part to a 13 × 9-

inch rectangle. Line bottom and sides of a 13 × 9-inch baking pan with waxed paper. Place rolled dough on waxed paper in baking pan. Spread ⅔ cup of the apricot preserves over dough. Sprinkle 1 cup of the walnut mixture over apricot preserves. Drizzle 4 teaspoons of the honey over walnuts. Roll second part of dough to a 13 × 9-inch rectangle. Place on top of first filling layer; press gently to smooth. Repeat filling over second dough layer. Repeat with third layer of rolled dough and remaining filling ingredients.

Bake for 40 to 45 minutes, or until top layer of filling becomes a glossy golden brown. Let cool. To serve, cut into squares. ❧

Apple Sponge Cake

Biszkopt z Jablkarni

It's best to prepare the crust dough a day in advance.

Makes 1 large cake

Crust

    1 cup all-purpose flour

    ½ cup butter or margarine

    1 egg yolk

    1 tablespoon powdered sugar

    1 teaspoon vanilla extract

Apple Mixture

    8 large Granny Smith apples, peeled, cored, sliced

    ¼ cup water

    1 cup sugar

    1 tablespoon cornstarch

    1 teaspoon vanilla extract

Sponge Cake Batter

    3 eggs

    3 tablespoons sugar

    1 teaspoon vanilla extract

    2 tablespoons all-purpose flour

    1 teaspoon baking powder

    3 tablespoons dry bread crumbs

Prepare dough for Crust: Place flour, butter, egg yolk, powdered sugar, and vanilla in a medium bowl. Combine all ingredients, working them to a stiff dough with your hands.

Form into a ball. Cover with plastic wrap and refrigerate overnight.

Preheat oven to 400°F (205°C). Grease a 13 × 9-inch baking pan. On a floured surface, roll out the chilled dough to a rectangle large enough to line bottom and sides of the prepared baking pan. Carefully line pan with dough rectangle. Bake for 10 minutes. Let cool.

Prepare Apple Mixture: Place apples and water in a large pot. In a small bowl, combine sugar and cornstarch. Add sugar mixture and vanilla to apples. Bring apple mixture to a boil over medium heat, stirring frequently. Cook for 15 minutes, stirring gently. Remove apple mixture from heat and let cool.

Prepare Sponge Cake Batter: Place eggs, sugar, and vanilla in a large bowl. With an electric mixer, beat egg mixture until smooth and glossy. Sift flour and baking powder into egg mixture. Mix until smooth.

Preheat oven to 350°F (175°C). Sprinkle bread crumbs evenly over baked Crust. Spoon Apple Mixture over bread crumbs. Spoon cake batter over Apple Mixture. Smooth cake batter with a wide spatula. Bake for 1 hour, or until golden brown. Cool before serving. ⚜

Apple Bars
Szarlotka Krucha

These are a classic companion to tea or coffee in Polish homes.

Makes 16 to 20 servings

4 cups all-purpose flour
1 teaspoon baking powder
1 cup plus 2 tablespoons powdered sugar
1½ cups plus 2 tablespoons unsalted butter or margarine
6 egg yolks
2 tablespoons sour cream
8 medium tart apples, peeled, sliced
¼ cup water
1 tablespoon ground cinnamon
1 cup granulated sugar
2 tablespoons potato starch or cornstarch
3 tablespoons lemon juice
3 tablespoons dry bread crumbs

Sift flour, baking powder, and the 1 cup powdered sugar into a large bowl. Cut butter into small pieces; work into flour mixture until mixture resembles coarse crumbs. Add egg yolks and sour cream; work into a firm dough. Press into a ball. Divide dough in half. Cover and refrigerate half the dough; freeze the other half.

To make filling, place apples and water in a large saucepan. Cover and cook over medium heat for 15 minutes. Add cinnamon and granulated sugar. Combine potato starch and lemon juice. Stir into apple mixture. Cook until apple mixture boils and thickens, 2 to 3 minutes, stirring frequently.

Preheat oven to 350°F (175°C). Grease a 13 × 9-inch baking dish. On a lightly floured board, roll refrigerated dough part into a 13 × 9-inch rectangle. Place rolled dough in greased baking dish. Sprinkle bread crumbs over rolled dough. Pour apple mixture on top of crumbs; smooth out apple mixture. Grate frozen dough over apple mixture in an even layer.

Bake for 55 to 60 minutes, or until golden brown. Cool in pan on a rack. Sift the 2 tablespoons powdered sugar on top. To serve, cut into squares. ❖

Apple Tart

Szarlotka

The more tart the apples, the better flavor you will have.

Makes 20 to 24 servings

2½ cups all-purpose flour
½ teaspoon salt
¾ cup unsalted butter or margarine
5 egg yolks
¾ cup sugar
2 pounds tart cooking apples, peeled
½ to 1 cup sugar
1 teaspoon ground cinnamon
1 teaspoon vanilla extract
3 tablespoons dry bread crumbs
Sugar to taste

In a large bowl, combine flour and salt. Using a pastry blender or 2 knives, cut butter into small pieces; add to flour. Work butter into flour until mixture resembles coarse crumbs. Add egg yolks and ¾ cup sugar; knead into a smooth dough. Cover loosely with foil or waxed paper. Refrigerate for 30 minutes.

Preheat oven to 350°F (175°C). Grease a 13 × 9-inch baking pan. Divide dough into 2 equal parts. On a lightly floured surface, roll 1 part dough to a 13 × 9-inch rectangle. Place rolled dough on bottom of greased pan; pat smooth. Bake for 10 to 15 minutes, or until crust sets. Reduce oven temperature to 325°F (165°C).

Using a coarse blade, grate apples into a large bowl. Add ½ to 1 cup sugar, depending on tartness of apples. Stir in cinnamon and vanilla. Sprinkle bread crumbs evenly over crust in pan. Spoon apple filling over bread crumbs; smooth apples with a spoon. Roll second part of dough to a 13 × 9-inch rectangle. Cut into thin strips. Crisscross dough strips over apple filling. Sprinkle a little sugar on top of dough strips. Bake for 50 minutes, or until dough strips are browned. Cool on a rack. To serve, cut into squares. ❖

Jam Crescents
Rogaliki

Serve this rich, delicate cookie for any tea or special event.

Makes 60 to 70 cookies

8 egg yolks
1 tablespoon sour cream
1½ cups unsalted butter or margarine, at room temperature
4½ cups all-purpose flour
1 teaspoon baking powder
1⅓ cups sifted powdered sugar
About ½ cup apricot preserves
½ cup finely chopped walnuts
1 egg, lightly beaten

In a large bowl, beat together egg yolks, sour cream, and butter. Combine flour, baking powder, and powdered sugar. Blend dry ingredients into egg yolk mixture, forming a smooth dough. Press dough into a ball. Cover and refrigerate overnight.

Preheat oven to 350°F (175°C). Divide dough into quarters. On a lightly floured board, roll out one-fourth of dough into a rectangle about ¼ to ⅛ inch thick. Using a sharp knife or pastry wheel, cut into 3-inch triangles. Spread ¼ teaspoon of the preserves over each triangle. Sprinkle ½ teaspoon of the walnuts over preserves. Starting at short side of triangle, roll jelly-roll style.

Place on an ungreased baking sheet, curving dough to create a crescent shape. Repeat with remaining dough, preserves, and walnuts. Brush crescents lightly with egg. Bake for 6 to 8 minutes, or until tops become golden. ♣

Sweet Crisps
Chrusciki

These impressive sweet treats will melt in your mouth.

Makes 12 to 14 dessert servings

1 cup all-purpose flour
3 egg yolks
3 tablespoons sour cream
1 teaspoon vanilla extract
1 tablespoon vodka, whiskey, or vinegar
Pinch salt
Vegetable shortening or oil
Powdered sugar

Place flour in a medium bowl; make a well in center. Add egg yolks; work with your fingertips until blended. Add sour cream, vanilla, vodka, and salt. Blend well. On a lightly floured board, work mixture into a smooth dough. Dough should have tiny air bubbles throughout. Cover and refrigerate for later use. For immediate use, on a lightly floured board, roll out dough to about $\frac{1}{16}$ inch thick. Slice into 1½-inch-wide strips. Cut strips diagonally into 5-inch lengths. Cut 1-inch slits lengthwise in center of each strip. Pull 1 end of a strip back through slit so strip resembles a bow tie. Repeat procedure with remaining strips. In a large skillet, heat 1-inch-deep vegetable shortening or oil to 375°F (190°C), or until a 1-inch bread cube turns golden brown in 50 seconds. Deep-fry strips less than 1 minute, or until golden, turning once. Drain on paper towels; let cool. Dust with powdered sugar. Serve at room temperature.

Variation
Crispy Rosebuds: Instead of strips, cut dough into an even number of 2½-, 2-, and 1½-inch circles. Score each dough circle 6 to 8 times by slitting from edge to center about two-thirds the distance. Use 1 of each size to prepare each rosebud.

In a small bowl, lightly beat 1 egg white. Dab egg white on center of 1 large scored dough circle. Press medium scored circle onto first, centering. Dab egg white onto center of medium circle. Press on smallest circle. Repeat procedure until all rosebuds are made. Drop completed rosebuds into hot oil as above, smallest circle down. Fry as above. Decorate with a dusting of powdered sugar and by placing a maraschino cherry, dab of jam, or dollop of chocolate in center of top. ♣

Sponge Cookies
Biszkopty

These crisp, light cookies are especially delicious when served with ice cream.

Makes about 40 cookies

5 eggs, separated
1 cup sugar
1½ cups all-purpose flour
½ teaspoon salt

Preheat oven to 350°F (175°C). Grease 2 baking sheets or line with parchment paper.

In large bowl of an electric mixer, beat egg yolks and sugar until creamy, about 5 minutes on high. Combine flour and salt in a sifter. Continue to beat egg mixture on high, gradually sifting in flour mixture.

In a medium bowl, beat egg whites until stiff but not dry. Beat one-third of egg whites into batter. Fold in remaining egg whites until smooth with no egg white showing.

Spoon mixture into a pastry bag fitted with a large plain nozzle. Pipe 3½-inch-long cookies onto prepared baking sheets, leaving space between each cookie for spreading during cooking. Bake for 15 to 20 minutes, or until light golden. Cool cookies on baking sheets for 3 to 4 minutes. Transfer to a rack to cool completely.

Cream Tarts
Babeczki Smietankowe

This is a favorite dessert of children, especially when decorated with funny faces.

Makes 18 to 20 tarts

Individual Tart Shells
½ cup sugar
1 cup butter or margarine, at room temperature
1 egg
2 cups all-purpose flour

Cream Filling
6 eggs
1 tablespoon vanilla extract
¼ cup all-purpose flour
⅔ cup sugar
2 cups milk
Raisins, cherries, or walnut halves (optional)

Prepare Individual Tart Shells: Preheat oven to 350°F (175°C). Beat together sugar, butter, and egg until light and fluffy. Gradually add flour until blended and smooth. Turn out dough on a lightly floured surface. Divide dough into 3 parts. Pinch off small pieces and press into 2½-inch tartlet pans, or roll 1 dough portion until ¼ to ⅜ inch thick. Using a small plastic lid or inverted bowl as a guide, cut 4-inch circles. Set scraps aside. Roll out remaining portions of dough, cutting as many circles as possible. Gently knead all dough scraps together. Roll out and cut more circles for a total of 18 to 20 circles. Gently press each circle into a 2¾-inch muffin cup, making evenly spaced tucks around edge of each circle. Bake for 20 minutes, or until golden. Cool in pans for 2 to 3 minutes on a rack. Remove from pans; cool completely on rack.

Prepare filling: In top of a double boiler, beat eggs and vanilla together. Combine flour and sugar; add gradually to egg mixture, beating constantly.

In a medium saucepan, bring milk to a boil over medium-high heat. Remove from heat as soon as milk begins to boil. Add milk to egg mixture, a little at a time, until all milk is added. Bring 2 to 3 inches water to a boil in bottom of double boiler. Cook egg mixture over boiling water, stirring constantly, until smooth, glossy, and the consistency of pudding, about 15 minutes. Let cool. Spoon equal amounts of cooled custard into each cooled baked tart shell. Decorate with raisins as desired. Refrigerate tarts until chilled before serving. ❖

Flavored Fruit Gel

Kisiel

A refreshingly cool, thick dessert, this has a delicious fruit flavor.

Makes 4 to 6 servings

> 1 quart fresh raspberries or red currants
> 1½ cups cold water
> 2 tablespoons sugar
> 1½ tablespoons potato starch or cornstarch

Place fruit and 1 cup of the water in a medium saucepan. Bring to a boil over medium-high heat. Reduce heat to low. Simmer, uncovered, for 20 minutes, stirring occasionally. Stir sugar into simmering berry mixture.

In a small bowl, blend potato starch and the remaining ½ cup cold water. Strain cooked berries through a fine-mesh strainer into a medium bowl; extract cooking juices, then discard seeds and pulp. Stir starch mixture into strained cooking liquids. Place strained mixture in a medium saucepan. Bring to a boil over medium heat, stirring constantly. Pour into small serving dishes or pudding dishes. Refrigerate for 2 or more hours before serving. ❖

METRIC CONVERSION CHARTS

When You Know	Symbol	Comparison to Metric Measure	To Find	Symbol
Teaspoons	tsp.	5.0	milliliter	ml
Tablespoons	tbsp.	15.0	milliliters	ml
Fluid Ounces	fl. oz.	30.0	milliliters	ml
Cups	c.	0.24	milliliters	l
Pints	pt.	0.47	liters	l
Quarts	qt.	0.95	liters	l
Ounces	oz.	28.0	grams	g
Pounds	lb.	0.45	kilograms	kg
Fahrenheit	F	5/9 (after subtracting 32)	Celsius	C

Fahrenheit to Celsius

F	C
200–25	95
220–225	105
245–250	120
275	135
300–305	150
325–330	165
345–350	175
370–375	190
400–405	205
425–430	220
445–450	230
470–475	245
500	260

Liquid Measure to Milliliters

1/4 teaspoon	=	1.25 milliliters
1/2 teaspoon	=	2.50 milliliters
3/4 teaspoon	=	3.75 milliliters
1 teaspoon	=	5.00 milliliters
1 1/4 teaspoons	=	6.25 milliliters
1 1/2 teaspoons	=	7.50 milliliters
1 3/4 teaspoons	=	8.75 milliliters
2 teaspoons	=	10.0 milliliters
1 tablespoon	=	15.0 milliliters
2 tablespoons	=	30.0 milliliters

Liquid Measure to Liters

1/4 cup	=	0.06 liters
1/2 cup	=	0.12 liters
3/4 cup	=	0.18 liters
1 cup	=	0.24 liters
1 1/4 cups	=	.30 liters
1 1/2 cups	=	.36 liters
2 cups	=	.48 liters
2 1/2 cups	=	.60 liters
3 cups	=	.72 liters
3 1/2 cups	=	.84 liters
4 cups	=	.96 liters
4 1/2 cups	=	1.08 liters
5 cups	=	1.20 liters
5 1/2 cups	=	1.32 liters

INDEX

Marianna Olszewska Heberle, a native of Suwalki, Poland, currently resides with her husband and three daughters in Erie, Pennsylvania. She was brought up on a small farm in a village in northeastern Poland, not far from the Russian border. There she frequently assumed household cooking responsibilities while her parents and brothers worked in the fields. Often, Marianna cooked at her grandmother's side, learning many old-time recipes and techniques at an early age.

ABOUT THE AUTHOR

After moving to the United States, Marianna worked as a supermarket delicatessen operator, taught Polish cooking classes, cooked for and catered private dinner parties, wrote and published *A Pierogi Handbook*, and gave lectures and cooking demonstrations at the Cracow Festival at Alliance College, the college of the Polish National Alliance in Cambridge Springs, Pennsylvania.

Marianna has been an active participant in many culinary and Polish-sponsored functions both within and outside of her community, such as the Pennsylvania Farm Show, and Philadelphia's The Book and the Cook Festival, and frequently shares both her culinary skills and the results of those skills with close friends and acquaintances. Through this book, she hopes to share some of Poland and its native cuisine with you.